SpringerBriefs in Economics

SpringerBriefs present concise summaries of cutting-edge research and practical applications across a wide spectrum of fields. Featuring compact volumes of 50 to 125 pages, the series covers a range of content from professional to academic. Typical topics might include:

- A timely report of state-of-the art analytical techniques
- A bridge between new research results, as published in journal articles, and a contextual literature review
- A snapshot of a hot or emerging topic
- An in-depth case study or clinical example
- A presentation of core concepts that students must understand in order to make independent contributions

SpringerBriefs in Economics showcase emerging theory, empirical research, and practical application in microeconomics, macroeconomics, economic policy, public finance, econometrics, regional science, and related fields, from a global author community.

Briefs are characterized by fast, global electronic dissemination, standard publishing contracts, standardized manuscript preparation and formatting guidelines, and expedited production schedules.

More information about this series at http://www.springer.com/series/8876

László Szerb • Eva Somogyine Komlosi
Zoltan J. Acs • Esteban Lafuente
Abraham K. Song

The Digital Platform Economy Index 2020

Springer

GEDI
THE GLOBAL ENTREPRENEURSHIP AND DEVELOPMENT INSTITUTE

László Szerb
Faculty of Business and Economics
University of Pécs
Pécs, Hungary

Zoltan J. Acs
Schar School of Policy and Government
George Mason University
Arlington, VA, USA

Abraham K. Song
Assistant Professor of Public Policy
Pepperdine University
Graduate School of Education and Psychology
Los Angeles, CA, USA

Eva Somogyine Komlosi
Faculty of Business & Economics
University of Pecs
Hosszúhetény, Baranya, Hungary

Esteban Lafuente
Department of Management
Universitat Politècnica de Catalunya
Barcelona, Spain

ISSN 2191-5504 ISSN 2191-5512 (electronic)
SpringerBriefs in Economics
ISBN 978-3-030-89650-8 ISBN 978-3-030-89651-5 (eBook)
https://doi.org/10.1007/978-3-030-89651-5

This Springer imprint is published by the registered company Springer Nature Switzerland AG
The registered company address is: Gewerbestrasse 11, 6330 Cham, Switzerland

Preface

In April 2020, the GEDI launched a preliminary report about measuring the digital entrepreneurship ecosystem. Over time, the concept has gone through several iterations and is now ready to be published. Like the Global Entrepreneurship Index products, we are planning to continue this research and publish yearly reports.

The application of big data, new algorithms, and cloud computing is creating a global digital platform economy built around platform companies. The Digital Platform Economy Index (DPE Index) integrates two separate but related literatures on ecosystems, namely, the digital ecosystem and the entrepreneurial ecosystem. This new framework situates digital entrepreneurship within the broader context of users, platforms, and institutions, such that two biotic entities (users and agents) actuate individual agency, and two abiotic components (digital infrastructure and digital platforms) form the external environment. If a country builds out its digital ecosystem, there is no guarantee that it will be exploited by existing firms. Startups' adoption of new technologies because of an entrepreneurial ecosystem is also uncertain. For technology to be introduced successfully, the digital ecosystem and the entrepreneurial ecosystem must be developed simultaneously.

To measure the size of the digital platform economy, we have developed the DPE Index, a multidimensional, composite indicator. The DPE Index framework includes 12 pillars that integrate the digital and the entrepreneurship ecosystems. Here, we report on the DPE Index, the four sub-indices, and the 12 pillar values for 116 countries; we also provide a cluster analysis based on the 12 pillars. The developed Anglo-Saxon and Nordic countries lead the DPE Index ranking, followed by other European and Asian nations, New Zealand, and Australia. Many mid-developed European, Asian, and Latin American countries and a group of oil-rich countries (i.e., Bahrain, Oman, Qatar, Saudi Arabia, and United Arab Emirates) report below-average DPE Index scores, while developing economies in Africa, Asia, Europe, and Latin America are in the group of poorly performing countries. The DPE Index results reveal that most European Union (EU) member states (22 out of 27) are on or above the trend line; however, except for The Netherlands, they are far below the two top DPE performers (the USA and the UK).

While it is useful to identify the common components of the digital platform economy ecosystem, policy recommendations should be individual and tailor-made. This report offers policy recommendations on three levels and are based on the harmonization of digital and entrepreneurship ecosystem components, and the 12 pillars. First, we identify the countries that are below the development-implied trend line, and which should spend more on improving their digital platform economy ecosystem. Next, we examine the balance of the digital and the entrepreneurship ecosystems. Imbalances could result in asynchronous operation, thus a healthy digital platform economy requires both digital and entrepreneurial ecosystem components. Finding the weak components of the digital platform economy ecosystem constitutes the third-level policy propositions. Weak components, called bottlenecks, could prevent a country from fully exploiting the possibilities provided by the stronger elements of the ecosystem. We center our focus on the European countries, including showing that the EU has paid a price for BREXIT. The UK is a dominant player in the digital platform economy arena, and it will be difficult to find a substitute.

Pécs, Hungary — László Szerb
Baranya, Hungary — Eva Somogyine Komlosi
Arlington, VA, USA — Zoltan J. Acs
Barcelona, Spain — Esteban Lafuente
Los Angels, CA, USA — Abraham K. Song

About The Global Entrepreneurship and Development Institute

The Global Entrepreneurship and Development Institute (The GEDI Institute) is the leading research organization in advancing knowledge on the relationship between entrepreneurship, economic development, and prosperity. The Institute, headquartered in Washington, DC, was founded by leading entrepreneurship scholars from George Mason University, the University of Pécs, Imperial College London, and the London School of Economics. For a long time, the Institute's flagship project was the Global Entrepreneurship Index (GEI), a breakthrough advance in measuring the quality and dynamics of entrepreneurship ecosystems at a national and regional level. The GEI project was completed in 2019 and a new index developed. Incorporating changes caused by the information technology revolution and globalization, the Institute has turned its focus to the connection between digitalization and entrepreneurship. This newly developed measure, called the Digital Platform Economy Index, is a country-level composite indicator of the global digital ecosystem. We hope it will be as helpful as the GEI.

Schar School of Policy and Government
George Mason University
Arlington, VA, USA

Zoltan J. Acs

Contents

1 Introduction 1

2 The Concept of the Platform-Based Ecosystem: The Digital Platform Economy 3

3 From Concept to Measurement: The 12 Pillars and their Measurement 7
3.1 The Structure of the DPE Index 8
3.2 The Description of the Pillars and their Components 8
3.2.1 Digital Access 9
3.2.2 Digital Freedom 10
3.2.3 Digital Protection 11
3.2.4 Digital Literacy 12
3.2.5 Digital Openness 12
3.2.6 Digital Rights 13
3.2.7 Networking 14
3.2.8 Matchmaking 15
3.2.9 Financial Facilitation 15
3.2.10 Digital Adoption 16
3.2.11 Technology Absorption 17
3.2.12 Technology Transfer 17

4 The Digital Platform Economy Index: Country Rankings and Clustering 19
4.1 Country Ranking: DPE Index and Sub-Index Analysis 19
4.2 Country Grouping: Pillar-Level Analysis 25
4.3 Regional Performance 26

5 Improving the Digital Platform Economy: Policy Suggestions 31
5.1 The Progress of the Digital Platform Economy in Terms of Economic Development 34
5.2 Digital and Entrepreneurship Ecosystem Investigations and Policy Recommendations 35

5.3 The Increase of the DPE Index Scores: Optimizing Additional Resources 40
5.4 The Full Profile of a Country: The Case of the United Kingdom . . . 42

6 Summary and Conclusion 49

The Applied Indicators in the Digital Entrepreneurship Index 51

The Calculation of the DPE Index and the Components Scores 61

References 65

List of Figures

Fig. 2.1 The platform-based ecosystem. Source: Song (2019, p. 576) 4

Fig. 3.1 The structure of the DPE index 9

Fig. 4.1 Digital platform economy index, 2020 map 27
Fig. 4.2 Selected European countries by pillar 28

Fig. 5.1 The top 100 platform companies around the world (October 2020) 32
Fig. 5.2 The regional distribution of the unicorns ($1 billion startups) around the world (February 2021) 33
Fig. 5.3 The connection between development and the DPE Index scores (third-degree polynomial adjustment) 35
Fig. 5.4 The six groups of countries based on the difference between the digital ecosystem and entrepreneurship ecosystem scores and the deviation from the implied development trend line 36

List of Tables

Table 2.1 Keys to building a sustainable digital platform economy 6

Table 4.1 The Digital Platform Economy Index ranking of the countries, 2020 20
Table 4.2 The four sub-index scores and ranking of the top 25 countries 23
Table 4.3 The four groups of countries and average pillar scores based on the 12 pillars 25
Table 4.4 Top scores by region 27

Table 5.1 Policy recommendations with respect to the DPE Index trend-line deviation and the digital ecosystem/entrepreneurship ecosystem mix 37
Table 5.2 The DPE Index pillar scores of selected countries 40
Table 5.3 Digital platform economy optimization analysis for selected European countries: The distribution of additional resources for a 10% increase of the DPE Index scores 42
Table 5.4 Digital platform economy profile of the United Kingdom 44
Table 5.5 United Kingdom's policy optimization simulation: The allocation of additional resources among the pillars to reach a 10% increase in DPE Index score 45
Table 5.6 The four sub-indices of selected EU countries, the UK, and the US 45

Table A.1 The applied indicators of the DTI sub-index 52
Table A.2 The applied indicators of the DUC sub-index 54
Table A.3 The applied indicators of the DMSP sub-index 56
Table A.4 The applied indicators of DTE sub-index 58

Chapter 1
Introduction

In one of the most interesting articles on the Information-Technology Revolution (ITR), Hobijn and Jovanovic (2001) argued that the arrival of the ITR in the 1970s created a need for new firms (Greenwood & Jovanovic, 1999). Technology breakthroughs favor the formation of new firms for three reasons: They provide awareness and skills, vintage capital, and vested interests. The stock market incumbents of the day were not ready to implement new digital technologies, thus it took new firms to bring the technology to market after the mid-1980s.The stock prices of incumbents fell immediately. New venture capital flowed to startups that built the new industries in the USA, but this did not occur in Europe (Gompers & Lerner, 2001). Between 1980 and 2020, the U.S. stock market increased 30-fold. The five most valuable public companies in the USA in 2020—Apple, Amazon, Microsoft, Facebook, and Google—are valued at or near $1 trillion each.[1] Many of them are "matchmaker" businesses whose core competency is the ability to match one group of users with another by reducing transaction costs.

The ITR is about digital technology and the representation of information in bits (Shannon, 1948), which reduces the cost of data storage, computation, and transmission. Digital economics examines whether and how digital technology changes economic activity (Goldfarb & Tucker, 2019). Digital technologies reduce five distinct types of costs that affect economic activities: search, replication, transportation, tracking, and verification. Reducing search costs leads to more matching and peer-to-peer platforms that increase the efficiency of trade. Most of the major technology firms can be seen as platform-based businesses. There are two main reasons why digital markets give rise to platforms (Jullien, 2012). First, platforms facilitate matching because they provide a structure that can take advantage of low search costs to create efficient matches. Second, platforms increase the efficiency of trade through lower search costs, lower reproduction costs, and lower verification costs

[1] See https://www.androidcentral.com/alphabet-becomes-fourth-trillion-dollar-company; accessed 2/14/2020.

L. Szerb et al., *The Digital Platform Economy Index 2020*, SpringerBriefs in Economics, https://doi.org/10.1007/978-3-030-89651-5_1

(Goldfarb & Tucker, 2019, p. 13). The literature on digital economics has examined how digital technology changes economic activity; less has been written about how it affects the platform economy.

In this report, we provide a framework to promote better understanding of the platform economy, multi-sided platforms, and the platform-based ecosystems. The term "digital platform economy" was coined by Kenney and Zysman (2016, p. 62) as "a more neutral term that encompasses a growing number of digitally enabled activities in business, politics, and social interaction (Peitz & Waldfogel, 2012). If the industrial revolution was organized around the factory, today's changes are organized around these digital platforms, loosely defined." Advancements in information and communication technologies (ICT) opened a pathway for these businesses. More specifically, platforms are enabled by technological openness (architectural interface specification) and organizational openness (governance), both of which are mediated by the platform owner. This rise of multi-sided digital platforms as avenues for value creation, appropriation, and innovation is commonly known as platformization.

While Kenney and Zysman (2016) focused on the nature of work, this study focuses on the changing structure of the economy. In the platform economy, costs are reduced not by management but by digital platforms—that is, technology. Therefore, one hallmark of the platform economy is the creation of markets where they did not exist by increased matching and the spread of platform-based businesses (Cusumano et al., 2019). A question that has received little attention is how the ITR has affected the organization of the firm. In other words, how do lower search costs affect firm organization? Lower search and verification costs have led to a new form of organization—the platform-based ecosystem.

The newly created Digital Platform Economy Index (DPE Index) provides a country-level measure of the digital platform economy. The DPE Index consists of twelve pillars and four sub-indices: Digital Multisided Platforms, Digital User Citizenship, Digital Technology Entrepreneurship, and Digital Technology Infrastructure. These sub-indices include the key economic, business, social, and policy issues: competition, privacy, innovation, and security, respectively (Sussan & Acs, 2017; Song, 2019). Building on the National Systems of Entrepreneurship methodology (Acs et al., 2014), we calculate the DPE Index scores for 116 countries. A major advantage of this index is that it allows us to make international comparisons about digital efficiency across countries and over time.

Following the conceptual description of the digital platform economy, in Chap. 3 we provide a detailed description of the structure of the DEP Index, focusing on the 12 pillars. In Chap. 4, we report the DPE Index scores and ranking for 116 countries, which represent all regions of the world. We use cluster analysis to classify the countries into four groups, as well as a regional-level analysis based on the World Bank classification. Our index-building methodology makes it possible to identify the critical weak points in the efficient operations of the platform economy ecosystem. In Chap. 5, we offer policy recommendations that are individual, country sensitive, and include the overall ecosystem development, the balance of the digital and entrepreneurship components, and the identification of bottlenecks across the 12 pillars. Finally, using the new measure of the DPE Index, we examine the EU's platform economy dilemma.

Chapter 2
The Concept of the Platform-Based Ecosystem: The Digital Platform Economy

The transition from a managed economy in the twentieth century to a platform economy in the twenty-first century is perhaps best summed up by Historian Niall Ferguson (2019) in his book *The Square and the Tower: Networks and Power from the Freemasons to Facebook*. Ferguson starts his story in Italian city states, where a tower sits in the middle of the town square. The tower represents the hierarchy, and the crucial incentive that favored the hierarchical order was that it made the exercise of power more efficient. Moreover, absolutism could be a source of social cohesion. Yet the defect of autocracy is obvious, too. No individual, no matter how talented, has the capacity to contend with all the challenges of imperial governance, and almost no one is able to resist the corrupting temptations of absolute power. Networks are changing the power balance of firms, governments, and countries (Root, 2020).

One of the main institutional differences, if not the most significant, between the managed economy and the platform economy is the role of the platform-based ecosystem. While there is an extensive literature on entrepreneurial ecosystems, this literature is misleading. As many have argued (Stam, 2015), entrepreneurial ecosystems appear to be a regional or local phenomenon.[1] However, when one compares entrepreneurial ecosystems with platform-based ecosystems, including the role of digital technology, the platform-based ecosystem becomes global in nature with billions of users and millions of agents (Sussan & Acs, 2017). Moreover, these ecosystems are developed and nurtured not by regions or governments but by platform organizations. Ecosystem governance—that is, the rules for who gets on a platform and what constitutes good behavior—is determined by the platform firm owners.

Sussan and Acs et al. (2017) were among the first to recognize this shortcoming in the ecosystem literature. They observed that a significant gap exists in the conceptualization of entrepreneurship in the digital age precisely because it ignored the

[1] Malecki (2018) emphasized the regional aspect of entrepreneurial ecosystems; Cavallo et al. (2018) focused on present debates and future directions.

L. Szerb et al., *The Digital Platform Economy Index 2020*, SpringerBriefs in Economics, https://doi.org/10.1007/978-3-030-89651-5_2

fundamental role of knowledge as a resource in the economy. To address this gap, Sussan and Acs et al. (2017) proposed the platform-based ecosystem, a novel framework also known as the Digital Entrepreneurial Ecosystem (DEE), which integrates two separate but related ecosystem literatures, the digital ecosystem and the entrepreneurial ecosystem literature. This new framework situates the platform-based ecosystem in the broader context of users, agents, infrastructure, and institutions such that two biotic entities (users and agents) actuate individual agency, whereas two abiotic components (digital technology and digital institutions) form the external environment. Song (2019) further refined the DEE framework and expanded it to include multi-sided platforms.

The DPE framework consists of four concepts: (1) Digital User Citizenship (DUC), which includes users on the demand side and the supply side; (2) Digital Technology Entrepreneurship (DTE), which includes app developers and various agents that contribute to entrepreneurial innovation, experimentation, and value creation on platforms; (3) Digital Multi-sided Platforms (DMP), which orchestrate social and economic activities between users and agents; and (4) Digital Technology Infrastructure (DTI), which pertains to all regulations that govern technical, social, and economic activities of the digital technology (Fig. 2.1).

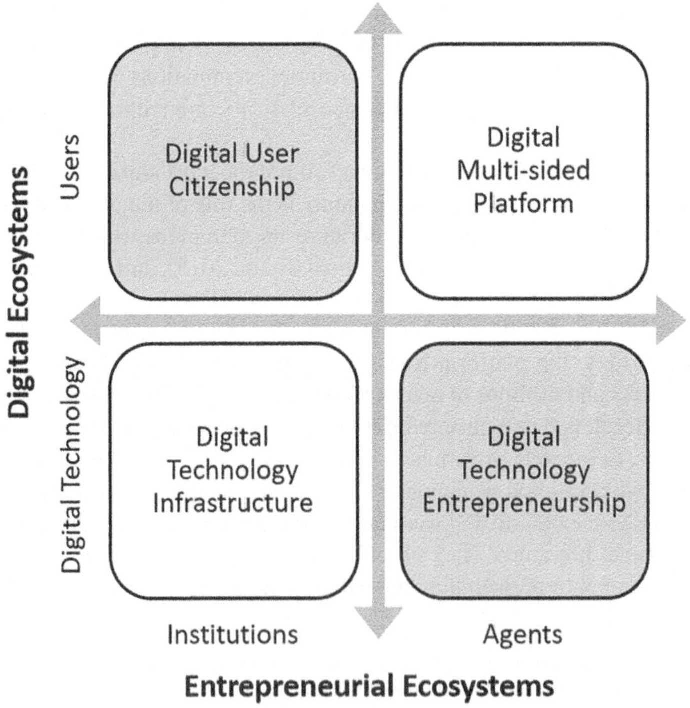

Fig. 2.1 The platform-based ecosystem. Source: Song (2019, p. 576)

First, protecting users' privacy is critical for a healthy and active DUC. If the public trust is eroded, the sustainability of the DEE suffers. Erosion of trust in platforms can lead to a decline in user activity or membership. For example, Facebook's scandal involving Cambridge Analytica exposed millions of users' data and became a watershed moment that prompted more government regulation of the internet to protect consumer privacy. Since then, Facebook has experienced a steady decline of daily active users in Europe.

Second, DTE brings forth entrepreneurial innovation and thereby increases platform efficiency. The larger the user base, the larger the market segments and niches. A good platform sponsor provides boundary resources that ease the entrepreneurial innovation process and offers a fair profit-share plan. Some critics have complained over the years that Apple's high developer commissions and fierce control over its app store can limit experimentation, entrepreneurial innovation, and value creation.

Third, DMP are the key organizational innovation of the ITR (Rochet & Tirole, 2003, 2006; Gawer, 2009; Evans & Schmalensee, 2007, 2016). Saadatmand et al. (2019) describe "digital platforms as an emergent organizational form characterized by technology and social processes." The monopolistic behavior of DMP will stifle competition, innovation, and entrepreneurial activities, resulting in a welfare loss for consumers and society as a whole. For example, European regulators have penalized Google for three anti-trust violations: for unfairly pushing its apps on smartphone users and blocking rivals; for using its search engine to steer consumers to its own shopping platforms; and for blocking its rivals from placing advertisements on third-party websites.

Fourth, DTI enables the platform economy to operate. Digital infrastructure represents the technology of the digital age, along with the rules and regulations that govern its use. This technological infrastructure is crucial to the smooth working of the DPE, which is responsible for keeping the digital economy open and secure. Chinese smartphone and telecommunication giant Huawei has been accused of being controlled by the Chinese government and of using its equipment to spy on companies and countries. These allegations about control, ownership, and fraud have raised questions as to whether Huawei should be allowed to build the world's 5G mobile infrastructure. While Huawei has defended itself as an open, transparent, and trustworthy company, it remains to be seen how global users and governments will respond (Table 2.1).

In addition to the aforementioned conditions, one must point out the role digital finance plays in building a sustainable DPE. Secure and reliable digital technologies are a necessary precondition for online financial transactions to flourish. Migration to a cashless society is a necessary first step that users will be inclined to take only if there are tangible benefits. One such benefit is lower transaction costs—the seamless payment experience between users and agents. Digital finance has also transformed capital markets. One rather remarkable trend is the emergence of crowdfunding as an alternative method to raising capital. Crowdfunding is a concerted effort to source funding online, much like knowledge commons efforts to source knowledge online. Another important trend is the rise of digital platforms, many of which are unicorns. Startups are reaching a $1 billion or even $10 billion

Table 2.1 Keys to building a sustainable digital platform economy

Digital user citizenship	Digital multi-sided platform
Because public trust is a prerequisite to user participation in the digital economy, a sustainable DPE will require that terms of user privacy be clearly laid out and upheld by a social contract. • Key word: "Privacy". • Example: Facebook.	For a sustainable DPE, digital platforms should be restrained from participating in monopolistic behavior that stifles market competition, innovation, and entrepreneurial activity. • Key word: "Competition". • Example: Google.
Digital technology infrastructure	**Digital technology entrepreneurship**
For a sustainable DPE, governments must be responsible for enacting and enforcing rules and regulations to discourage destructive activities that undermine data security and encourage productive activities. • Key word: "Security". • Example: Huawei.	For a sustainable DPE, third-party agents engage in entrepreneurial innovation and knowledge exchange that closes the gap between supply opportunity and demand need on platforms that increase platform efficiency. • Key word: "Efficiency". • Example: Apple.

valuation (e.g., decacorns) at a faster pace: the average time for a US technology company to go public has gone from 11 years in 1999 to 4 years in 2011. The formation of megafunds, such as the Softbank's $100 billion Vision Fund, and the availability of venture capital increasingly leave little incentive for platform startups to go public. Behind this is the fact that demand-side driven businesses tend to take a long time to develop a sustainable revenue model; going public would subject them to scrutiny and pressure could drive down the value. In short, finding sustained long-term growth remains elusive.

Chapter 3
From Concept to Measurement: The 12 Pillars and their Measurement

While ecosystem theories and concepts have a relatively long history with both entrepreneurial ecosystems (Acs et al., 2017) and digital ecosystems (Li et al., 2012; Weill & Woerner, 2015), the digital entrepreneurship ecosystem and a platform-based economy concepts have emerged only recently (Elia et al., 2020; Nambisan, 2017; Sahut et al., 2019). Moreover, measurements are lagging behind conceptual developments. Some argue that all ecosystems are exclusive, as each has its unique component structure, strengths, and weaknesses. Consequently, case studies are more appropriate than simple or composite indicators to describe the ecosystem phenomenon (Isenberg, 2010; Spigel, 2017). While we agree that the specifics of each ecosystem can be viewed up close, when looking from a certain distance, one can recognize the common structures and features (Szerb et al., 2019). Accurate measurements are vital for three reasons. First, solid policy recommendations should be based on appropriate measures. Second, one can recognize the relative development of a particular unit by comparing it to other units' rankings and index scores. And third, an ecosystem's strengths and weaknesses can be identified from a benchmarking perspective.

While measures of digital and entrepreneurship ecosystems have been available for some time, there is only one country-level measure, the European Index of Digital Entrepreneurship Systems (EIDES) (Autio et al., 2018, 2019). EIDES has its theoretical roots in the entrepreneurship ecosystem concept, where the entrepreneurship ecosystem pillars are contextualized by their digital counterparts. This notion reflects the general use of digitalization of digital technologies in particular. The DPE Index differs from EIDES, in that the latter conceptualizes entrepreneurship ecosystems based on three business-development stages (stand up, start up, and scale up), whereas the former focuses on the context of users, agents, digital technologies, and institutions to fully capture the systemic developments, as identified by Jovanovic (1982, 2001). Furthermore, the DPE Index is centered around

L. Szerb et al., *The Digital Platform Economy Index 2020*, SpringerBriefs in Economics, https://doi.org/10.1007/978-3-030-89651-5_3

platformization, rather than solely on the use or application of digital technologies. Finally, EIDES is used only for EU member countries, while the DPE Index can compare EU countries to other nations.[1]

3.1 The Structure of the DPE Index

The DPE Index proposed in this study measures the DPE at the country level. Figure 3.1 pictures the DPE Index structure, including the four frameworks, called sub-indices. All four frameworks include three components that reflect the most important aspects of DTI, DUC, DMP, and DTE. Each pillar has two types of components, called variables (Fig. 3.1). For example, the digital rights pillar variables include institutions and digital technology; and the digital adoption pillar variables are digital technology and an agent.

The pillar variables include 2-5 indicators that represent the lowest level of our composite indicator. Our indicator selection criteria are based on the following:

1. Potential to link theoretically or at least logically to the particular digital or entrepreneurship variable.
2. The selected indicator's clear interpretation and explanatory power.
3. Potential duplication of the indicators is avoided.

In building our composite indicator, we applied a total of 61 indicators. We believe this number is sufficient to describe the complex phenomenon of the digital platform economy while also avoiding including too many indicators, which could lead to interpretation problems.

3.2 The Description of the Pillars and their Components

In this section, we provide a short view of each of the four sub-indices and the 12 pillars, as well as their measurement. The full description of the 61 indicators applied and their sources can be found in Appendix A.

Digital Technology Infrastructure "addresses the coordination and governance needed to establish a set of institutional standards" (Sussan & Acs, 2017, p. 64) that are related to digital technology.

---

[1] For other entrepreneurship ecosystem measures, see the Global Entrepreneurship Index, its regional counterpart the regional Entrepreneurship and Development Index, Kauffmann's entrepreneurship ecosystem, and the Startup Genome's Global Startup Ecosystem model-based measures. Digital measures can be divided into maturity/readiness, transformation, and complex indices. The best-known composite digital index is the European Union's Digital Economy and Transformation Index (DESI). Others are the Mastercard and the Fletcher School at Tufts University's Digital Evolution Index, and the Economic Intelligence Unit's Inclusive Internet Index.

	Sub-indices	Pillars	Variables (entrepreneurship/digital)
DIGITAL PLATFORM ECONOMY	Digital Technology Infrastructure	Digital access	*Digital access institutions*
			Digital access Digital technology
		Digital freedom	*Digital freedom institutions*
			Digital freedom Digital technology
		Digital protection	*Digital protection institutions*
			Digital protection Digital technology
	Digital User Citizenship	Digital literacy	*Digital literacy institutions*
			Digital literacy Users
		Digital openness	*Digital openness institutions*
			Digital openness Digital technology
		Digital rights	*Digital rights institutions*
			Digital rights Digital technology
	Digital Multi-sided Platform	Networking	*Networking agents*
			Networking users
		Matchmaking	*Matchmaking agents*
			Matchmaking users
		Financial facilitation	*Financial facilitation agents*
			Financial facilitation users
	Digital Technology Entrepreneurship	Digital adoption	*Digital adoption agents*
			Digital adoption Digital technology
		Technology absorption	*Technology absorption agents*
			Technology absorption Digital technology
		Technology transfer	*Technology transfer agents*
			Technology transfer Digital technology

Fig. 3.1 The structure of the DPE index

3.2.1 Digital Access

Digital access refers to the level of access citizens have to the digital infrastructure, including computers, the internet, and various digital tools (tablets, laptops, mobile phones, etc.). Without proper access, individuals cannot participate in the digital world. The digital divide refers to the cultural groups or counties that do not have proper or equal access to digital tools (Van Dijk, 2017). The first level of the digital divide was initially observed in terms of gender, age, race, and disability (Friemel, 2016), but it now also includes the gap between developed and developing countries. A large proportion of developing country populations still have no access to the internet, which makes it impossible for them to enjoy the benefits of digital revolution (West, 2015).

However, digital inequality can occur even for those with access to digital content when they cannot access particular information. This second level of the digital divide is associated with the lack of "ability to efficiently and effectively find information on the Web" (Hargittai, 2002). This can create material, immaterial, and educational types inequality (Ghobadi & Ghobadi, 2015), and can reinforce or even exacerbate social inequalities (Robinson et al., 2015). A third degree of the digital divide was identified recently as inequality in the tangible outcomes of internet use (Scheerder et al.Van Dijk, 2017).

In the DPE, the institutional aspect of digital access is captured by two proxy indicators, the technical and the organizational sub-indices from the Global Cybersecurity Index. While these indicators do not really measure government efforts to increase digital access and reduce the digital divide, we assume that government security efforts could be positively associated with these two issues, including developing technical institutions and institutions that coordinate cybersecurity policy and strategy. The digital infrastructure aspect of digital access is more straightforward, including the three indicators of fixed broadband internet subscriptions, international internet bandwidth, and the percentage of individuals using a computer.

3.2.2 Digital Freedom

Digital freedom reflects how much freedom a government and its institutions provide in developing digital infrastructure. A typical example of hampering such development is restricting the use of the internet or internet services for security or political reasons (Weidmann et al., 2016). ICT-enabled services helped to organize both civil society and revolutionary movements in several countries, including Iran, Indonesia, Kyrgyzstan, Kuwait, Malaysia, and Turkey (Howard, 2010). Milner (2006) argued that democratic institutions facilitate the spread of the internet, whereas autocratic ones restrict it.

Another aspect of digital freedom is the potential monopolization of the digital infrastructure players (Nuechterlein & Weiser, 2007). Economies of scale are important drivers of digital infrastructure development, and network effects are vital in the digital platforms (Hindman, 2018). The limited number of service providers could be a sign of attempts to monopolize control and/or to restrain particular users (Moore, & Tambini, D. (Eds.)., 2018; Wentrup & Ström, 2017). Bock et al. (2014) claim that the EU has been lagging behind Asian and North American countries in providing advanced digital networks, mainly due to regulatory deficiencies. Maintaining sustainable infrastructure competition should be an important focus for EU regulatory bodies.

In the DPE, the infrastructure is measured by three indicators. From Freedom House we use two indices: Freedom of the press and Freedom in the World. This later includes a measure of political rights and civil liberties. The potential monopolization of the digital infrastructure is measured by the World Economic Forum (WEF) Network Readiness Index, which assesses internet and telephone infrastructure. The digital infrastructure is measured by the number of internet domains from Global Innovation Index and Webhosting. Since they are absolute numbers we have standardized them by the size of population.

3.2.3 Digital Protection

Digital protection captures the degree to which laws and regulations protect users from piracy and cybercrime. While openness and freedom are important aspects of the digital infrastructure, exposure to cyberattacks and violation of digital property rights could undermine its development. Herhalt (2011) categorized cyberattacks as financial scams, computer hacking, downloading pornographic images from the internet, virus attacks, e-mail stalking, and creating websites that promote racial hatred. The widening use of digital technology and online services has provided new opportunities—e-business, e-commerce, e-learning, e-banking, e-government—while also creating new challenges to security (Kundi & Akhtar, 2014; Lampson, 2004). Moreover, the growing reliance on the digital infrastructure increases its vulnerability and could do serious damage in almost every aspect of life, from basic services like electricity and water to transportation, education, and health-care systems (Johnson, 2016). Security imposes increasingly high costs on private users, businesses, and other organizations (Whitman & Mattord, 2012), including governments, which also are the target of attacks. As the cost of defending the digital infrastructure has been rising, internet or online piracy and the violation of copyrights have forced governments to create new law enforcement methods, such as the US Digital Millennium Copyright Act (Chaudhry et al., 2011).

The borderless cyberspace makes it difficult to track the source of crimes and identify culprits (Herhalt, 2011). The lack of access to computer experts also makes it difficult to fight against cybercrime, primarily but not exclusively in the less developed countries (Kundi & Akhtar, 2014). Recently, the Trump administration was urged to engage in a more aggressive and active cyber defense (Rosenzweig et al., 2017).

In the DPE, the infrastructure is measured by the legal sub-index of the Global Security Index and the Corruption Perception Index from Transparency International. The digital part of the digital protection pillar is proxied by the WEF Network Readiness Index software piracy rate.

Digital User Citizenship "addresses the explicit legitimization and implicit social norms that enable users to participate in digital society" (Sussan & Acs, 2017, p. 64). While DTI components aim to capture the role of institutions in terms of the digital infrastructure, the focus here is the effect institutions have on users, governments in particular, as they are a key influence on digital literacy. Although maintaining privacy is a key component of effective DUC and privacy is a widely investigated issue, it is difficult to quantify. Hence, we can use only partially appropriate proxy indicators.

3.2.4 Digital Literacy

Digital literacy refers to citizens' ability to use computers, the digital infrastructure, and digital platforms. Without such skills, people cannot take full advantage of the digital infrastructure. Literacy in a broad sense refers to skills or competences (Williams, 2003), but a narrower interpretation is having operational capabilities, such as "understanding ICT terminology, the ability to use basic features of software tools such as word-processors and spreadsheets; and the ability to save data, copy and paste, manage files, and standardize formats within documents." Advanced literacy "includes the use of search engines and databases, and the ability to make more advanced use of software tools" (Buckingham, 2006, p. 266).

An extended definition includes literacy in various areas: ICT and other technologies, information and media, visual and communications (Goodfellow, 2011, p. 133). Literacy is also used in a broader context that reflects the ability to understand, evaluate, and interpret information provided by the digital infrastructure, most importantly by the internet (Baron, 2019; Njenga, 2018). As more and more young children use and rely on the internet, protection from harmful online content has become an important issue in education (Poore, 2015). Internet users are increasingly exposed to fake news, dis- and -misinformation, and manipulation (Morgan, 2018; Weeks & Gil de Zúñiga, 2019). The 2016 US presidential campaign and the UK Brexit vote induced new research into the spread of fake news and false information (Persily, 2017; Rose, 2017).

From the user side in the DPE, we use two indicators: the WEF measure of digital skills among the population, and the number of search-engine users in a country, as reported by Bloom Consulting. From the institutional side we use two WEF education indicators: the quality of education, and internet access in schools.

3.2.5 Digital Openness

Digital openness reflects to how well a country's institutions support the reach and the use of digital infrastructure. Access to and the free use of information are vital for any society (Peters & Roberts, 2015). The creator of the World Wide Web, Berners-Lee (2009) was one of the first to urge governments to provide open-access data on the internet so users could exploit the full potential of digitization. The general development of the digital infrastructure, ability to connect to the internet, and the use of ICT, including various digital devices, enable users and agents to freely access digital information, which requires the support of government institutions and regulations. Legislation also should support interaction between the users and agents of e-commerce and e-transactions via the various platforms available.

In the DPE, the digital infrastructure is proxied by the percentage of individuals and households having access to the internet. The institution side of the pillar is measured by an indicator reflecting to the laws relating to the use of ICT and by the more complex Global Cyberlaw Tracker.

3.2.6 Digital Rights

Digital rights reflect the human and legal rights that make it possible for citizens to use the digital infrastructure, while at the same time protecting their privacy. Human rights include the right of free opinion and expression, as reinforced by the Vienna Declaration and Programme of Action in 1993. According to Klang and Murray (2005), human rights also include the free communication that is the central element of the information society. Limitless and borderless participation are important factors in having access to the information society offers and in respecting human rights. At the same time, all actors should take appropriate action to prevent the use of digital sources and technologies for illegal, abusive, criminal, or terrorist purposes. Since the beginning of the information age and the internet, privacy and the ability to control one's personal information have been of central interest (Smith et al., 2011; Bélanger & Crossler, 2011). Several researchers have observed contradicting behavior among internet users: while there is increasing concern about privacy, individuals are ready to share or sell their personal information for little or no compensation (Kokolakis, 2017; Kummer & Schulte, 2019).

The appearance of new digital communication tools and technologies opens up new fronts in the effort to balance and maintain easy access, privacy, and security, all at the same time. The millions of users of social networks are at the forefront of the privacy issue (Hajli & Lin, 2016). Users were alarmed when it came to light that Facebook passed the personal information of more than 87 million users to Cambridge Analytica (Isaak & Hanna, 2018), and the company's current practice of canceling users and censoring harmful content has raised a whole new set of concerns about the violation of privacy (Alkire et al., 2019). The increasing use of mobile applications (Christin et al., 2011), online finance and banking (Roca et al., 2009), and the internet of things (Pasquier et al., 2018) challenges the access and the privacy of users, governments, and digital infrastructure developers.

In the DPE, the institutional aspect of digital rights is captured by personal rights measure via the Global Talent Competitiveness Index, fundamental rights via the Rule of Law index, and property rights via the Property Rights Alliance. The digital aspect is proxied by a Kaspersky-based variable that includes the Net infection rate of the internet and internet censorship and surveillance data from Wikipedia. While the infection rate is generally related to security, we use it here as a proxy for privacy.

Digital Multi-sided Platforms are where digital technology users and agents of the entrepreneurship ecosystem meet. DMP serves as an "intermediary for [the] transaction of goods and services, and also [as] a medium for knowledge exchange that enables and facilitates experimentation, entrepreneurial innovation, and value creation" (Song, 2019, p. 4). In the DMP sub-index, we capture only a few characteristics of multi-sided platforms (MSP). From a country perspective, the two most important features of MSP are networking and competition. The effect of virtual networks is the main part of the networking pillar. The matchmaking pillar focuses on catching the user's contribution and the competitive push of startups. The third pillar emphasizes the financial potential of MSP that is vital to the digital entrepreneurship ecosystem.

3.2.7 Networking

The networking pillar aims to grasp the network effects and other external effects of MSP. Network effect is a kind of externality that occurs when the value of the product or service depends on the number of users (Shapiro & Varian, 1999). In the case of MSP, the value of the service to each member increases as the number of users rises. In the early phase of a platform launch, the attraction of both sides is vital. If there is a shortage of sellers, buyers may not find the platform attractive, and a lack of buyers discourages sellers from joining—a "chicken-and-egg problem" (Hagiu, 2014; Evans & Schmalensee, 2016).

Researchers have identified two kinds of effects: the same-side or direct effect, when users value the presence of similar users, and the cross-side or indirect effect, when users value the increased number of the agent side on the platform (Evans, 2013; McIntyre & Srinivasan, 2017). Social media platforms like Facebook are good examples of the direct effect, Uber of the indirect effect. Network effects can be further strengthened by high multi-homing and switching costs (Farrell & Klemperer, 2007; Hyrynsalmi et al., 2016). Both scale effect and scope effect are present in MSP, and platform providers can serve many different user groups with the same product (Lee, 2001). A supply side for scale effect could also emerge. According to Gawer (2014), modular design and the use of platforms make it possible for firms to gain economies of scope in innovation.

In the DPE, networking pertains to the application of various virtual networks and social media from the user side, and to business capabilities to provide goods and services via the internet from the agent side. We apply three partially overlapping indicators from the users side: the use of virtual social networks (ITU), social media penetration (Hootsuite), and the use of virtual professional networks (WEF). We apply two WEF-related indicators from the agent side, the ICT use of business-to-business transactions, and the business-to-customer internet use.

3.2.8 Matchmaking

In the matchmaking components, we aim to capture MSP business models that are different from earlier models. Traditional business models are based on a chain of vertically integrated firms. In MSP, both sides (supply and demand or buyers and sellers) become customers that interact with each other through the platform (Parker & Van Alstyne, 2014).

Matchmaking, or pairing the two sides of the platform, is not an easy task (Evans & Schmalensee, 2016). The key to matchmaking is the platform design, which includes the platform architecture, value creation logic, governance, and platform competition (Tura et al., 2018). Platform architecture refers to the core interaction of users and agents, including the openness of the platform and the potential restrictions on participation. For effective value creation and to maximize the network effect, the different shareholders' value positions should be understood. Pricing and revenue models are the key to value capture (Weyl, 2010). Platform designers also should deal with the potential effects of competition. In a turbulent environment, it is difficult to balance and maintain the ability to capture the market early, reach a critical mass, and prevent competitors from entering the market. Small changes in the platform design could produce significantly different results. MSP do not just connect supply and demand; they require the active participation of users who contribute to platform efficiency by commenting, evaluating, or correcting the content, goods, or services (Sussan & Acs, 2017).

In the DPE, this effect from the user side is captured by two indicators from INSEAD: Wikipedia's yearly edits, and video uploads on YouTube. From the agent side, we use the number of professional developers as a percentage of population and as a logarithmic of the country share. This latter indicator is supposed to grasp the size effect.

3.2.9 Financial Facilitation

Financial facilitation refers to various aspects of finance that rely on the digital technologies that fuel matchmaking-related startups, make financial transactions via the internet possible, and provide platforms for financial service providers and users. New technology trends such as artificial intelligence and machine learning, automation, big data, cloud computing, distributed ledger technology such as blockchain; new entrants such as mobile network operators, payment service providers, merchant aggregators, retailers, FinTech companies, neo-banks, and super platforms; and new business models have been reshaping the whole finance sector by providing cheaper, faster solutions, and new financial services (Gomber et al., 2018; Alt et al., 2018). Gomber et al. (2017) put digital finance business functions into six broad categories: digital financing, digital investments, digital money, digital payments, digital insurance, and digital financial advice.

In the DPE, we have only a few indicators available to measure the components of the financial facilitation pillar. From the user side, we apply four World Bank-related indicators, such as debit/credit cards used the internet to pay bills or buy something, used a mobile phone or the internet to access a financial institution account, and made or received digital payments. For the agent side we rely on three indicators: the depth of the capital market sub-index score from the Venture Capital and Private Equity Country Attractiveness Index, the standardized number of Fintech companies based on Dealroom data, and venture capital availability, from the WEF.

Digital Technology Entrepreneurship "is comprised of various third-party agents that partake in experimentation, entrepreneurial innovation, and value creation using hardware/software to build products that connect to platforms" (Song, 2019, p. 9). Baierl et al. (2019) describe digital entrepreneurship "as creating new ventures and transforming existing businesses by developing novel digital technologies or novel usage of such technologies … Additionally, digital technologies have become a new economic and social force for reshaping traditional business models, strategies, structures, and processes" (p. V). The first part of the definition refers to digital entrepreneurship as an output, the second part as a context (Elia et al., 2020). From another perspective, this differentiates two types of entrepreneurship: Schumpeterian and Kirznerian. Schumpeter (1934) entrepreneurship is referred to as "creative destruction." From the DPE side, Schumpeterian entrepreneurship is assumed to be an exogenous given, whereas DTE captures entrepreneurial efforts that contribute to a more efficient or novel use of digital technologies. This kind of entrepreneurship is usually labeled Kirznerian, or opportunity motivated entrepreneurship (Kirzner, 2015; Lafuente et al., 2020).

3.2.10 Digital Adoption

The digital adoption pillar components reflect entrepreneurial agents' basic ability to use digital technologies. By adopting advanced digital technologies, startups and existing businesses can increase their efficiency by reducing production, communication, and coordination costs (Goldfarb & Tucker, 2019; Sahut et al., 2019). This is particularly important for businesses in less developed countries, where advanced technology can reduce the physical distances between markets. Differences in digital and ICT capabilities could create a digital divide that would be a serious barrier to successful digital adoption (Fong, 2009; Cruz-Jesus et al., 2017). Several phases of digital adoption lead to digital maturity (Becker et al., 2009). Moreover, the degree and the content of digitization change over time; therefore, striving for maturity is a never-ending process rather than a static state (Kane et al., 2017). From 1990 to 2000, having a web presence, digital marketing, and digital selling were at the center of the digital transformation (Hull et al., 2007). Later, offering integrated solutions that included the strategy, the workforce, the culture, the technology, and the structure to meet the expectations of various stakeholders became the core of digital transformation and digital maturity (Kane et al., 2017).

The digital adoption pillar components capture the basic development of the digital infrastructure as measured by the electricity production (two indicators) and telephone network (three indicators) indicators. From the agent side of the digital adoption pillar, we use two proxies, one to measure the level of digitalization by computer software spending, and another to quantify the basic talents of the country workforce.

3.2.11 Technology Absorption

Technology absorption measures the extent to which entrepreneurial agents can absorb existing digital technologies. It requires recognizing useful, newly developed digital technologies and building them into the business model. While the focus in the digital adoption pillar is on relatively well-developed digital tools and methods, the emphasis here is on turning to newly created technologies that are less mature and riskier but could lead to more profitable business prospects. Digital technologies and the widely interpreted digital infrastructure provide new opportunities for entrepreneurs. Digital technologies enable the entrepreneur to experiment and to implement new business models (Baierl et al., 2019). Autio et al. (2018) identified three digitalization promoted affordances "that shape both the locus of entrepreneurial opportunities in the economy, as well as the effective practices to pursue such opportunities" (p. 74). These affordances are decoupling form and function; disintermediation, or shrinking the role of the intermediary in the value chain; and generativity, the ability to connect dispersed participants. According to Amit and Zott (2012), business model innovation occurs in three ways: introducing new business activity, altering the structure of the activities, and changing governance of the activities. The role of entrepreneurs is not only to recognize evolving opportunities provided by new technology but to exploit their value creation and build it into the business model (Elia et al., 2020; Steininger, 2019).

In the digital absorption pillar, the digital infrastructure component is captured by two indicators: the number of data centers from the Data Centers catalog, and the availability of latest technology from the WEF. The agent component is measured by a complex variable that includes the knowledge absorption capacity sub-index, and by two indicators reflecting the effects of ICT on new business and organizational models. All data are from the Global Innovation Index.

3.2.12 Technology Transfer

Technology transfer identifies another aspect of technology entrepreneurship, the ability to disseminate digital technologies. The speed at which a country can diffuse new technologies is an important factor in improving efficiency and development (Kiiski & Pohjola, 2002). Technological diffusion is a highly uneven process, and the success of laggard countries depends on how quickly their leaders can adapt new technology to a country-specific context (Andrews et al., 2015). Forming new firms plays an important role in the diffusion of new technologies although not all startups contribute equally to efficiency improvements (Lafuente et al., 2020).

The speed and depth of a country's technology transfer ability depend on its overall innovation capabilities. Innovation-based digital technology is different from classic innovation in several respects. Unlike traditional supply and demand models, the concept of open innovation describes digital innovation better (Chesbrough, 2006). Traditional innovation usually occurs in-house, while digital innovation relies increasingly on external actors and knowledge (Lund & Ebbesson, 2019). Moreover, digital innovation is a non-linear process wherein networks orchestrate ideas, technologies, tools, actors, and know-how (Lyytinen et al., 2016). Digital technologies enable connections between various heterogeneous actors with transaction costs close to zero.

Technology transfer is not a mechanical process; it requires tacit knowledge that is difficult to transmit. Incomplete knowledge spillover in digital technologies can slow regional growth (Batabyal & Nijkamp, 2016). Moving from adopting simple digital technology to more complex absorption and transfer demands advanced digital skills from both the entrepreneurs and their employees (Dede, 2010). Developing new skills and capabilities are key factors in successful knowledge spillover. It has been well-known for more than two decades that routine types of jobs and the associated skills are disappearing, and that digital technology increasingly demands new competencies (Murawski & Bick, 2017; Prensky, 2009). Voogt and Roblin (2012) identified the new competencies as transversal (can be applied in many fields), multidimensional (involving knowledge, skills, and attitudes), and higher order (reflecting the ability to solve complex problems in unpredictable environments). Communication and teamworking ability, as well as a solid understanding of the information exchanged, are also key to successful technology absorption (Elia et al., 2020).

An increasing number of tech startups and well-functioning innovation capacities are the key for a successful technology transfer. From the agent side of the technology transfer pillar, this influence is proxied by a Startup ranking -based indicator of the number of startups. The skill component is measured by the high-level skills sub-index from the Global Talent Competitiveness Report. From the digital infrastructure part of this pillar, we use two components: knowledge and technology output from the Global Innovation Index, and innovation capacity, which is a similar component from the Global Competitiveness Index. We are aware that these components are proxies, but data availability limited our choices.

Chapter 4
The Digital Platform Economy Index: Country Rankings and Clustering

In this section, we provide a basic analysis of digital entrepreneurship, which we called the DPE Index, for 116 countries from all continents and in all development stages. The calculation steps of the DPE Index are found in Appendix B.

4.1 Country Ranking: DPE Index and Sub-Index Analysis

According to Table 4.1, the USA leads the DPE Index 2020 ranking with a score of 85.0, followed by the United Kingdom (82.7), and The Netherlands (82.4). Of the top 10 countries, two are in North America (US and Canada) and seven in Europe (UK, Netherlands, Sweden, Switzerland, Norway, Denmark, and Finland); Australia ranks ninth. The next 10 countries, ranked 11-20, have a similar regional distribution: eight European countries (Ireland, Luxembourg, Germany, France, Iceland, Belgium, Estonia, and Austria), and New Zealand and Hong Kong. All of these countries are highly developed, innovation-driven economies. In contrast, the countries in the last 10 places (107-116) are less developed, resource-driven countries on the African continent, with the exception of Cambodia.

While the DPE Index score is useful in comparing a country's digital platform-based ecosystem performance to that of other nations, it does not reveal any of a country's strengths and weaknesses. For further details, we need to break down the components of the DPE Index. Table 4.2 presents the four sub-index scores and ranking of the top 25 countries.

The USA is first in the DMP and DTE sub-indices, sixth in the DUC, and second in the DTI. The best sub-index score for the US is 92.3 (DTE), the worst is 73.3 (DUC), a 20.6% difference. The UK's scores are even more balanced, ranging from its best of 84.8 (DUC) to its lowest of 81.3 (DTI). Some countries have greater

L. Szerb et al., *The Digital Platform Economy Index 2020*, SpringerBriefs in Economics, https://doi.org/10.1007/978-3-030-89651-5_4

Table 4.1 The Digital Platform Economy Index ranking of the countries, 2020

Rank	Country	DPE 2020	GDP 2017
1	United States	85	54,225
2	United Kingdom	82.7	39,753
3	Netherlands	82.4	48,473
4	Canada	78.2	44,018
5	Sweden	76.8	46,949
6	Switzerland	76.3	57,410
7	Norway	74.4	64,800
8	Denmark	71.1	46,683
9	Australia	69.3	44,649
10	Finland	68.9	40,586
11	Ireland	66	67,335
12	Luxembourg	65.6	94,278
13	New Zealand	65.3	36,086
14	Germany	64.4	45,229
15	France	63.6	38,606
16	Iceland	62.6	46,483
17	Belgium	62.5	42,659
18	Estonia	60	29,481
19	Hong Kong	58.5	56,055
20	Austria	57	45,437
21	Japan	56.8	39,002
22	South Korea	56.4	35,938
23	Israel	56.2	33,132
24	Singapore	55.8	85,535
25	Spain	53.5	34,272
26	Malta	53.4	36,513
27	Portugal	50.8	27,937
28	Czech Republic	48.9	32,606
29	Taiwan	47.1	50,294
30	Italy	46.1	35,220
31	Slovenia	45.1	31,401
32	Lithuania	44.3	29,524
33	Cyprus	44.3	32,415
34	United Arab Emirates	43.1	67,293
35	Latvia	42.8	25,064
36	Malaysia	42.1	26,808
37	Qatar	40.7	116,936
38	Chile	40.6	22,767
39	Poland	40.6	27,216
40	Slovakia	40.5	30,155
41	Hungary	38.4	26,778
42	Uruguay	36.3	20,551

(continued)

Table 4.1 (continued)

Rank	Country	DPE 2020	GDP 2017
43	Greece	35.9	24,574
44	Bulgaria	35	18,563
45	Croatia	34.8	22,670
46	Costa Rica	34.1	15,525
47	Romania	33	23,313
48	Russia	32.7	24,766
49	Turkey	32.3	25,129
50	Mauritius	32	20,293
51	Brazil	31.2	14,103
52	Argentina	30.4	18,934
53	Mexico	29.4	17,336
54	Ukraine	29.3	7894
55	Saudi Arabia	29.3	49,045
56	Oman	28.8	37,961
57	Montenegro	28.5	16,409
58	China	28.1	15,309
59	Colombia	28	13,255
60	Panama	28	22,267
61	Bahrain	27.6	43,291
62	Serbia	27.5	14,049
63	Thailand	27.2	16,278
64	Georgia	26.5	9745
65	South Africa	26.4	12,295
66	Macedonia	25.3	13,111
67	Jordan	25	8337
68	Armenia	25	8788
69	Moldova	24.4	5190
70	Morocco	24.4	7485
71	Philippines	24.3	7599
72	Azerbaijan	23.9	15,847
73	India	23.8	6427
74	Peru	23.6	12,237
75	Kazakhstan	23.5	24,056
76	Indonesia	23.1	11,189
77	Kuwait	22.8	65,531
78	Bosnia and Herzegovina	21.4	11,714
79	Ecuador	21.3	10,582
80	Tunisia	21.1	10,849
81	Albania	20.5	11,803
82	Vietnam	20.3	6172
83	Dominican Republic	19.8	14,601
84	Jamaica	19.7	8194

(continued)

Table 4.1 (continued)

Rank	Country	DPE 2020	GDP 2017
85	Egypt	19.5	10,550
86	Iran	19.5	19,083
87	Botswana	19.5	15,807
88	Namibia	18.3	9542
89	Sri Lanka	18.3	11,669
90	Lebanon	17.6	13,368
91	Kenya	17.5	2993
92	Mongolia	17.3	11,841
93	El Salvador	16.7	7292
94	Paraguay	15.6	8827
95	Guatemala	15	7424
96	Segal	14.5	2471
97	Pakistan	14	5035
98	Honduras	13.9	4542
99	Nigeria	13.7	5338
100	Zambia	13.4	3689
101	Algeria	12.5	13,914
102	Rwanda	11.9	1854
103	Nepal	11.6	2443
104	Kyrgyzstan	11.5	3393
105	Bangladesh	11.2	3524
106	Uganda	11	1698
107	Cameroon	10.8	3365
108	Mali	10.4	2014
109	Zimbabwe	10	1900
110	Cambodia	9.8	3645
111	Tanzania	9.8	2683
112	Malawi	9.8	1095
113	Benin	9.6	2064
114	Madagascar	7.3	1416
115	Burundi	6.9	702
116	Ethiopia	6	1730

Note: DPE = Digital Platform Economy index score; GDP = the per capita GDP of the country in purchasing power parity (World Bank, 2017) (https://data.worldbank.org/indicator/NY.GDP.PCAP.PP.KD)

variation. For example, ninth-ranked Australia is seventh in the DTI (78.2) but 18th in the DTE (57.0), a 27.1% difference. The balance for EU member countries is varied. While The Netherlands is first in the DTI (90.5), it is only fourth in the DUC (74.1), with a significantly lower score and 18% difference. Germany's major weakness is in the DMP, while France and Spain are more balanced.

Table 4.2 The four sub-index scores and ranking of the top 25 countries

DPEIndex Ranking	Country	Digital Technology infrastucture score	Digital Technology Infrastucture ranking	Digital user citizenship score	Digital user citizenship ranking	Digital multi-sided platform score	Digital multi-sided platform ranking	Digital technology entrepreneurship score	Digital technology entrepreneurship ranking
1	United States	86,9	2	73,3	6	87,5	1	92,3	1
2	United Kingdom	83,1	4	81,4	1	84,8	3	81,3	3
3	Netherlands	90,5	1	74,1	4	86,3	2	78,7	4
4	Canada	78,5	6	78,1	2	78,9	5	77,2	5
5	Sweden	79,4	5	73,9	5	79,5	4	74,4	6
6	Switzerland	77,9	8	72,9	7	69,4	9	84,9	2
7	Norway	83,6	3	76,6	3	73,5	6	63,8	12
8	Denmark	75,2	9	71,3	10	73,4	7	64,4	11
9	Australia	78,2	7	72,9	8	69,3	10	57,0	18
10	Finland	70,7	11	71,6	9	67,2	11	66,1	8
11	Ireland	64,8	17	64,3	15	65,4	14	69,6	7
12	Luxembourg	73,7	10	65,6	14	60,3	17	63,0	14
13	New Zealand	67,3	14	68,5	11	70,4	8	55,0	23
14	Germany	69,6	12	68,3	12	56,4	23	63,2	13
15	France	67,2	15	61,3	18	60,4	16	65,4	9
16	Iceland	65,4	16	53,8	22	65,6	13	65,4	10
17	Belgium	64,0	18	61,4	17	64,9	15	59,6	17
18	Estonia	63,7	19	63,5	16	57,5	22	55,2	21
19	Hong Kong	69,4	13	48,8	26	58,8	20	57,0	19

(continued)

Table 4.2 (continued)

DPEIndex Ranking	Country	Digital Technology infrastucture score	Digital Technology Infrastucture ranking	Digital user citizenship score	Digital user citizenship ranking	Digital multi-sided platform score	Digital multi-sided platform ranking	Digital technology entrepreneurship score	Digital technology entrepreneurship ranking
20	Austria	62,7	21	58,6	19	50,1	28	56,7	20
21	Japan	62,7	20	66,4	13	44,3	34	53,8	24
22	Korea	56,0	23	56,5	20	59,6	18	53,3	26
23	Israel	49,1	29	47,6	28	67,0	12	61,0	16
24	Singapore	56,6	22	46,7	30	58,6	21	61,2	15
25	Spain	52,3	27	55,1	21	52,6	25	53,8	25

4.2 Country Grouping: Pillar-Level Analysis

We have conducted a cluster analysis that shows common features and differences in the 12 pillars. The four-cluster group solution proved the most useful for our purposes. Table 4.3 shows a relative imbalance in the number of cluster members: Leaders consist of only 7 countries, Followers of 20, Gainers of 35, and Laggards number 54 countries. The differences among the groups in terms of the DPE Index mean score varies. The Leaders (DPE Index = 77.7) are ahead of the Followers (DPE Index = 61.3) by around 16 points, the Gainers (DPE Index = 35.9) are behind the Followers by around 25 points, and the Laggards (DPE Index = 17.4) are last, by roughly 19 points. The first six countries in the DPE Index ranking belong to the Leaders group, mainly North American and European (Nordic and Anglo-Saxon) nations. The Followers group contains only developed European and Asian countries and two developed Oceania countries, New Zealand and Australia. Gainers are geographically mixed, dominated by mid-developed European, Asian, and Latin American countries. Most oil-rich countries (i.e., Bahrain, Oman, Qatar, Saudi Arabia, and United Arab Emirates) also belong to this cluster. Laggards are formed from less-developed African and Asian countries, together with relatively poor European and Latin American nations.

Leaders: Canada, Iceland, Netherlands, Sweden, Switzerland, United Kingdom, USA;

Followers: Australia, Austria, Belgium, Denmark, Estonia, Finland, France, Germany, Hong Kong, Ireland, Israel, Japan, South Korea, Luxembourg, Malta, New Zealand, Norway, Singapore, Spain, Taiwan,

Gainers: Argentina, Bahrain, Brazil, Bulgaria, Chile, China, Costa Rica, Croatia, Cyprus, Czech Republic, Georgia, Greece, Hungary, Italy, Latvia, Lithuania,

Table 4.3 The four groups of countries and average pillar scores based on the 12 pillars

Categories/groups	Leaders	Followers	Gainers	Laggards
Digital Access	82.3	74.9	43.7	11.1
Digital Freedom	80.2	60.3	35.3	22.2
Digital Protection	88.3	74.2	37.5	14.6
Digital Literacy	77.4	59.2	33.6	24.1
Digital Openness	76.6	71.7	43.2	13.4
Digital Rights	68.5	62.8	36.3	22.2
Networking	84.1	64.2	37.2	19.1
Matchmaking	82.7	61.3	40.6	18.1
Financial Facilitation	79.3	70.1	38.3	16.8
Digital Adoption	81.8	63.0	39.0	18.6
Technology Absorption	83.3	59.1	34.4	22.9
Technology Transfer	82.0	63.2	35.8	20.6
Digital Platform Economy Index score mean	**77.7**	**61.3**	**35.9**	**17.4**
Number of cases	7	20	35	54

Macedonia, Malaysia, Mauritius, Mexico, Montenegro, Oman, Poland, Portugal, Qatar, Romania, Russia, Saudi Arabia, Slovakia, Slovenia, Turkey, Ukraine, United Arab Emirates; Uruguay;

Laggards: Albania, Algeria, Armenia, Azerbaijan, Bangladesh, Benin, Bosnia and Herzegovina, Botswana, Burundi, Cambodia, Cameroon, Colombia, Dominican Republic, Ecuador, Egypt, El Salvador, Ethiopia, Guatemala, Honduras, India, Indonesia, Iran, Jamaica, Jordan, Kazakhstan, Kenya, Kuwait, Kyrgyzstan, Lebanon, Madagascar, Malawi, Mali, Moldova, Mongolia, Morocco, Namibia, Nepal, Nigeria, Pakistan, Panama, Paraguay, Peru, Philippines, Rwanda, Senegal, Serbia, Sri Lanka, South Africa, Tanzania, Thailand, Tunisia, Uganda, Vietnam, Zambia, Zimbabwe.

The Leaders are best in all 12 pillar score averages. These are mainly rich Anglo-Saxon and Nordic countries with well-balanced digital entrepreneurship ecosystems. While they spend the most for digital protection, digital rights are their lowest value pillar. Only two small EU member countries (Netherlands and Sweden) are in this group. The Followers are also rich developed nations. Although some aspects of their digital entrepreneurship ecosystems are well developed (Digital Access, Digital Protection), they have relatively low scores on some pillars (Digital Literacy, Technology Absorption). The Gainers enjoy good digital technologies and citizens who are active users, but many aspects of their digital entrepreneurship ecosystems require considerable development. The Laggards are the lowest in every pillar score average. These countries lack digital infrastructure, good digital technologies, and active users. The last two group members are relatively homogenous, with minimal in-group differences. This is particularly true for the most populated Laggards cluster.

4.3 Regional Performance

For many countries, a regional benchmark is more relevant to identify best practices for fostering digital platform economy development. We follow the World Bank categorization in terms of regional membership. The map in Fig. 4.1 reveals significant differences in the digital platform economy development across regions and within regions. It is clear that developed countries in North America, Europe, and the Asia-Pacific region have more developed digital platform economies than nations in Latin America, South Asia, and Africa. Alterations within regions are associated with the countries' development: poorer countries typically have lower DPE Index scores, while richer countries have the highest scores in the DPE Index ranking.

Table 4.4 lists the regional leaders. In addition to the DPE Index scores and ranking, we provide the digital and entrepreneurship ecosystem component scores.

The US leads the world in entrepreneurship and is first in the North American region. Canada ranks fourth, making North America the world's most powerful region. The UK, second in the overall ranking, is first in the Europe-Central Asia region. Brexit cost the EU a dominant player in the digital platform economy game.

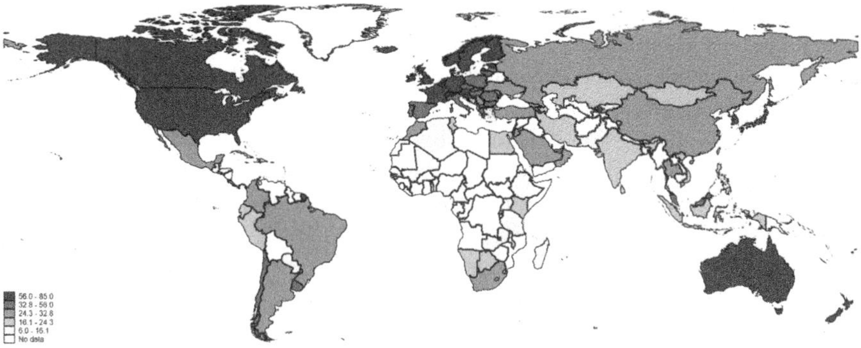

Fig. 4.1 Digital platform economy index, 2020 map

Table 4.4 Top scores by region

World Rank	Country	Region	GDP per Capita PPP 2019	Digital Ecosystem Component	Entrepreneurship Ecosystem Component	DPE Index
1	USA	North America	Int'l$54,225	87.4	90.9	85.0
2	United Kingdom	Europe / Central Asia	Int'l$39,753	85.2	86.8	82.7
9	Australia	East Asia / Pacific	Int'l$44,649	80.6	77.8	69.3
23	Israel	Middle East / North Africa	Int'l$33,132	71.5	74.8	56.2
38	Chile	Latin America / Caribbean	Int'l$22,767	60.3	60.3	40.6
50	Mauritius	Sub-Saharan Africa	Int'l$22,293	58.2	49.7	32.0
73	India	South Asia	Int'l$6427	46.4	33.9	23.8

Nordic countries and Switzerland have strong digital platform economies, while other large EU nations such as Germany and France lag behind the leading nations. Australia ranks first in the Asia-Pacific region, ahead of New Zealand and economic powerhouses Hong Kong, Japan, Korea, Singapore, and Taiwan. Israel ranks 23rd overall, tops in the MENA region ahead of Malta, the UAE, and Qatar. All other countries in the MENA region have DPE Index scores below 30. Chile ranks first in South and Central America and the Caribbean (38th overall), ahead of Uruguay and Costa Rica. In sub-Saharan Africa, Mauritius is the leader at 50th, ahead of South Africa and Botswana. Other sub-Saharan countries are at the bottom of the DPE Index ranking. There are only five countries in the South Asian region; ranking 73rd, India leads with a 23.8 DPE Index score, followed by Sri Lanka and Pakistan.

These low-middle income countries should increase their efforts to develop their digital platform economies.

A healthy digital entrepreneurship economy requires balancing the digital and the entrepreneurship components. In Table 4.4 we can see that most of the regional leaders have relatively well-balanced digital and entrepreneurship ecosystems. In the US and Israel the entrepreneurship component is slightly higher, while the digital component is more dominant in Australia. The UK and Chile seem to be well-balanced, whereas Mauritius and India have relatively well-developed digital ecosystems. However, their entrepreneurship ecosystems are less developed, which prevents them from fully exploiting the opportunities provided by their digital ecosystems.

We selected some European countries to represent within-region differences. Figure 4.2 shows five European countries—Austria, Greece, The Netherlands, Spain, and the UK—at the pillar level. We already have seen that the UK and The Netherlands lead the region and that other countries lag significantly behind. In the DTI components, the difference between the leaders and followers is clear for all three pillars: Digital Openness, Digital Freedom, and Digital Protection. Those differences are similar to the DUC pillars: Digital Literacy, Digital Access, and Digital

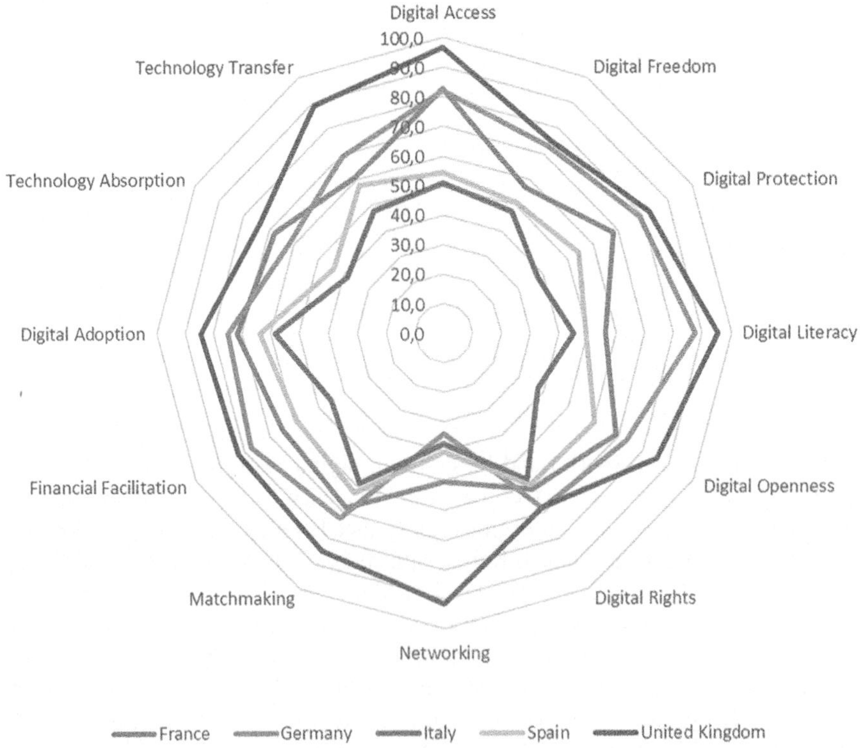

Fig. 4.2 Selected European countries by pillar

Rights. However, the differences are greater for literacy than for rights, as the EU has moved ahead on rights without regard for literacy. Among the DMP constituents, the real differences between leaders and followers are even greater. The UK and The Netherlands are almost 30 points higher than Spain and more than 35 points higher than Italy. The DTE differences are least for Digital Adoption and greatest for Technology Absorption.

Chapter 5
Improving the Digital Platform Economy: Policy Suggestions

Facilitating digital and entrepreneurship ecosystems is high on many government policy agendas. Many nations focus on developing the digital infrastructure, maintaining digital freedom and privacy, protecting users from cybercrime and piracy, improving the population's digital literacy, and supporting technology-related start-ups. However, enhancement of digital platform economies at the country level has been fragmented. Unfortunately, there is little understanding of how policies can foster this new type of economy most effectively. Some policies, such as the European Union Global Data Protection Regulation, have in fact had a negative effect on some information-sensitive business models (Hoofnagle et al., 2019). Those who want to regulate the digital platform ecosystem have to acknowledge that the most important platform companies are global and therefore call for global rather than local action. To highlight this, we report two interesting statistics.

It is immediately clear from Fig. 5.1 that the US and China dominate the platform landscape. Based on these top companies' market value, the US alone represents 66% of the world platform economy and 41% in terms of numbers. European platform-based companies play a marginal role, only 3% of the market value. Moreover, the distribution of the top 100 platform-based companies is uneven; the first 15 companies represent around 75% of the entire market value.

Of the 12 European platform-based companies, one is Norwegian, one Russian, two Dutch, two Swedish, three German, and three are in the UK. Just comparing platform-based ranking to the DPE Index ranking, the UK, The Netherlands, Sweden, and Norway are in the top ten, while Germany is 14th and Russia is 48th. It is immediately clear that a strong digital platform-based ecosystem alone is not enough to nurture multi-billion dollar platform-based companies. Country size also seems to matter. The UK has now left the EU, which reduced the number of top platform-based companies in the EU to seven, and only SAP is among the top 15. Perhaps a more unified EU would provide a more favorable environment for platform-based development.

L. Szerb et al., *The Digital Platform Economy Index 2020*, SpringerBriefs in Economics, https://doi.org/10.1007/978-3-030-89651-5_5

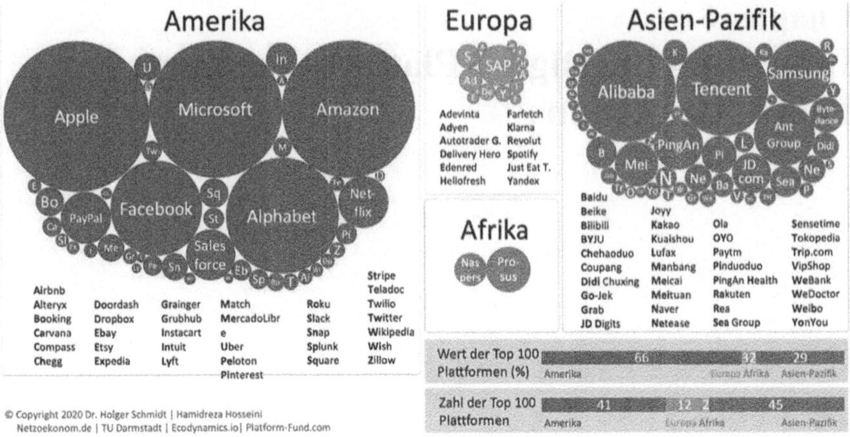

Source: https://www.netzoekonom.de/plattform-oekonomie/

Fig. 5.1 The top 100 platform companies around the world (October 2020)

The other interesting statistic is the number of startups valued at more than $1 billion, which are called unicorns.[1] As of February 2021, there were 546 unicorns, most of them technology-oriented and platform-based companies. The US dominates these rankings, with more than 50% of all unicorns, followed by China with 22%. Europe has 67 unicorns (12.2%) and the European Union is home to 36 (6.6%). Because of Brexit, the EU lost 26 unicorns. This picture is similar to the distribution of the 100 most important platform companies. Recent regulations, like the General Data Protection Regulation and the Global Data Protection Regulation, focus on ensuring that users know, understand, and consent to the data collected about them, which is not really helpful and not only limits the existing non-EU businesses but weakens EU-based startups. EU investigations of Microsoft, Alphabet/Google, Facebook, and other digital giants have only provided temporary protection for EU-based platform businesses (Fig. 5.2).

Therefore, national or EU-level regulators face dominant platform-based market players, most of which reside in the US. No dominant European player appears to be emerging in the platform business arena. Therefore, it is vitally important that the EU create an ecosystem that will enable local platform companies to become global actors.

The DPE Index is particularly helpful in identifying weaknesses in the ecosystem and providing solid policy suggestions. This index-building methodology relies on the Global Entrepreneurship Index techniques (Acs et al., 2014). Our policy propositions are based on two important postulates:

[1] See https://www.cbinsights.com/research-unicorn-companies

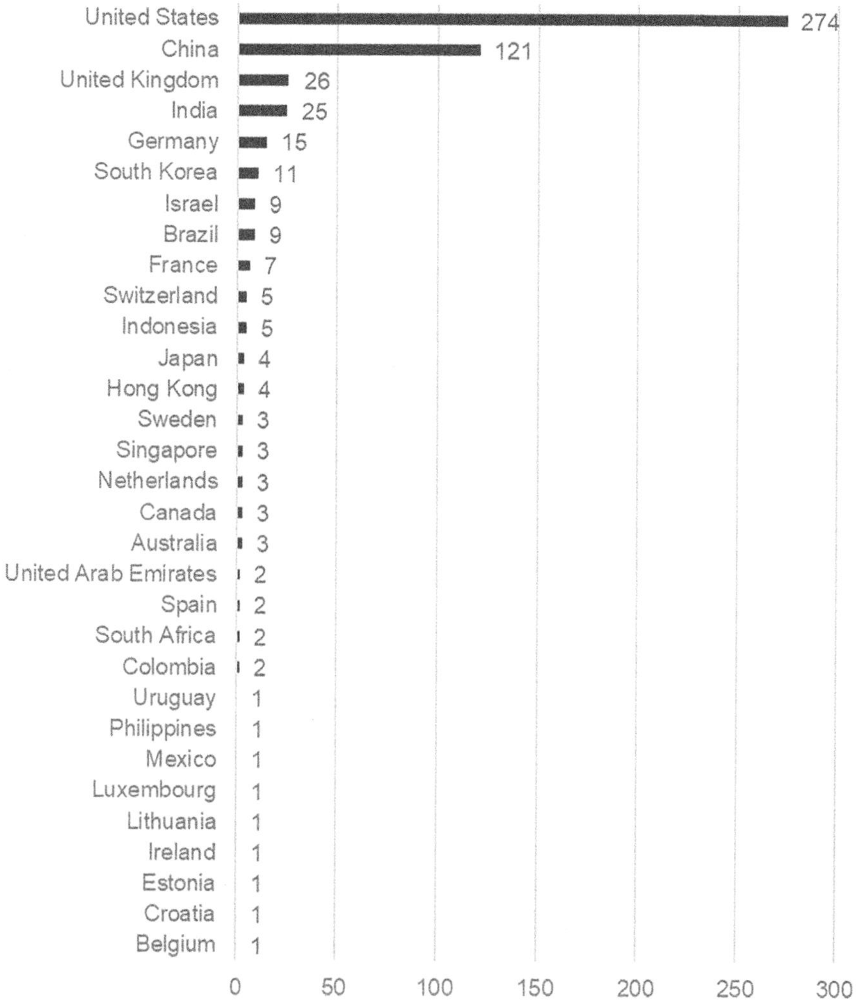

Source: Based on CBINSIGHTS data, author's own calculation (https://www.cbinsights.com/research-unicorn-companies)

Fig. 5.2 The regional distribution of the unicorns ($1 billion startups) around the world (February 2021)

1. Classic economic policy focuses on easing market failures. Ecosystem policies thus should center on alleviating system failures, such as weaknesses in the digital platform economic system.
2. Since the digital platform economy ecosystem is different in each country, policy recommendations should be country specific. There is no one-size-fits-all policy.

Two important index-building techniques make it possible to sharpen policy suggestions. Equalization of the pillar averages balances out the marginal effects of improvements, and the Penalty for Bottleneck (PFB) penalizes for bottlenecks in the 12 pillars in the digital platform economy.[2]

We provide policy recommendations in three ways. First, we study how advanced a country's digital platform economy ecosystem is. To do so, we calculate the implied development trend line and determine whether that country is above or below the line. This method takes into account the fact that countries have different levels of development. Therefore, we compare countries with similarly developed digital platform economies. Second, we examine the balance of the digital ecosystem and entrepreneurship ecosystem components. We believe that a healthy digital platform economy requires both ecosystem components to be at around the same level. If a country's digital component is more advanced, it should work to strengthen its entrepreneurship ecosystem and vice versa. Third, we identify the weak pillars in the digital platform economy ecosystem. We provide country-specific policy suggestions for distributing additional resources over the 12 pillars. We apply a 10% increase in the DPE Index scores. Our examples include the US, the UK, and select EU member countries.

5.1 The Progress of the Digital Platform Economy in Terms of Economic Development

There is a close connection between development and DPE Index scores: The Pearson correlation coefficient is 0.66 without the oil-rich countries or countries with a per-capita GDP higher than 65,000 International \$. The third-degree trend line shows an even closer connection, as pictured in Fig. 5.3.

The third-degree adjusted curve explains around 90% of the variation between development (measured by the per-capita GDP) and digital platform-based ecosystem (DPE Index). Note that it does not imply a causal relationship; we simply refer to the strong connection between development and the digital entrepreneurship ecosystem. Examining a particular country's position below or above the implied development trend line is more appropriate than simply comparing differently developed nations. For example, the USA has the highest DPE Index score (85.0) and is above the trend line, as are the United Kingdom, The Netherlands, and Sweden.

Of the large EU countries, only France and Spain are on or above the trend line. Germany and Italy both have lower DPE Index scores than implied by the trend line. Poorer EU countries like Poland and Greece have much lower DPE Index scores and are below the trend line.

[2] For further details see Acs et al. (2014).

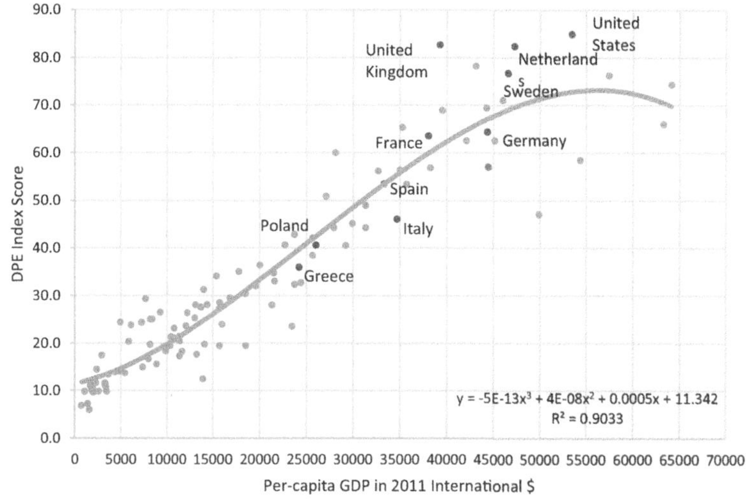

Note: The trend line is calculated without countries over 65 000 international $ per-capita GDP and without the oil-based economies of Bahrain, Kuwait, Oman, Qatar, Saudi Arabia, and United Arab Emirates.

Fig. 5.3 The connection between development and the DPE Index scores (third-degree polynomial adjustment)

5.2 Digital and Entrepreneurship Ecosystem Investigations and Policy Recommendations

Figure 5.4 groups the 116 countries into six quadrants. On the horizontal axis, the values are the difference between the DPE Index trend line and the actual DPE Index score in percentages. The DPE Index trend-line calculation is based on the per-capita GDP. The DPE Index trend line represents the best-fit power function, according to the following equation:

$$GDP\,\text{per capita} = -5E(-13) * DPE\,\text{Index}^3 + 4E(-08)\,DPE\,\text{Index}^2 + 0.0005 * DPE\,\text{Index} + 11.34 \tag{5.1}$$

On the vertical axis there is a difference between the between the digital ecosystem scores and the entrepreneurship ecosystem scores, in percentages.

We assume as a rule of thumb that a deviation of less than −5% from the implied development trend line or a −5% to 5% difference between the digital and entrepreneurship ecosystem scores is acceptable. If the deviation exceeds these values, then policy interventions are suggested (see Table 5.1 for details)

1. **Upper-right area (light blue color):** The country has a higher DPE Index score than the average similarly developed countries, and the digital ecosystem com-

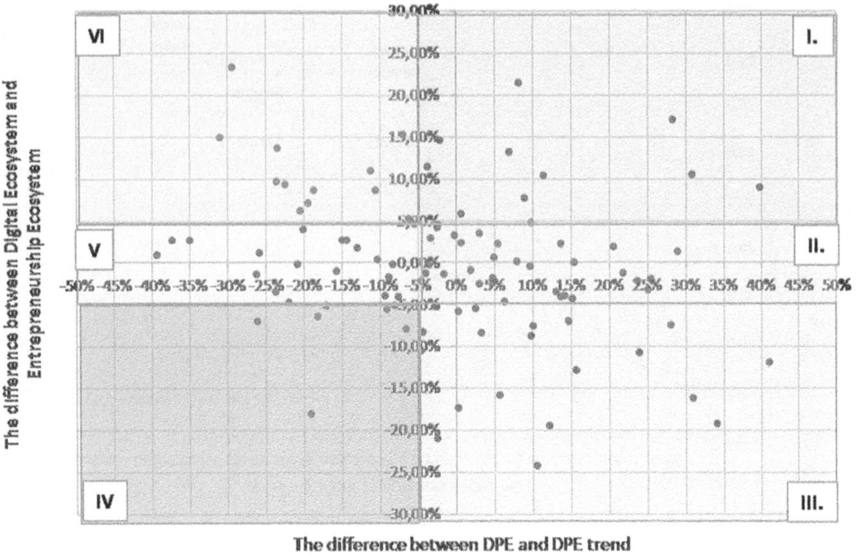

Fig. 5.4 The six groups of countries based on the difference between the digital ecosystem and entrepreneurship ecosystem scores and the deviation from the implied development trend line

ponent of this country is more than 5% higher than the entrepreneurship ecosystem component.

2. **Middle-right area (light green color):** The country has a higher DPE Index score than the average similarly developed countries. The digital ecosystem and the entrepreneurship ecosystem components share in this country are within the −5% to 5% range.
3. **Lower-right area (light orange color):** The country has a higher DPE Index score than the average similarly developed countries. The digital ecosystem component of this country is lower than the entrepreneurship ecosystem component.
4. **Lower-left area (medium grey color):** The country has a lower DPE Index score than the average similarly developed countries. The digital ecosystem component of this country is lower than the entrepreneurship ecosystem component.
5. **Middle-left area (light yellow color):** The country has a lower DPE Index score than the average similarly developed countries. The digital ecosystem and the entrepreneurship ecosystem components share in this country are within the −5% to 5% range.
6. **Upper-left area (light grey color):** The country has a lower DPE Index score than the average similarly developed countries. The digital ecosystem component of this country is higher than the entrepreneurship ecosystem component.

Table 5.1 Policy recommendations with respect to the DPE Index trend-line deviation and the digital ecosystem/entrepreneurship ecosystem mix

	Strong DE development (DE-EE difference is below −10%)	Some DE development (DE-EE difference is between −5% and 10%)	Keep balance between DE and EE (DE-EE difference is between −5% and 5%)	Some EE development (DE-EE difference is between 5% and 10%)	Strong EE development (DE-EE difference is above 10%)
Keep DPE development with GDP	Albania, Bosnia and Herzegovina, Colombia, Honduras, India, Indonesia, Peru, Philippines, Senegal, Ukraine, Vietnam	China, **Finland**, Jordan Pakistan, South Africa, Switzerland,	Argentina, Armenia, Australia, Bahrain, **Belgium**, Brazil, **Bulgaria**, Canada, Chile, Costa Rica, **Croatia, Czech Republic, Denmark**, Ecuador, Egypt, **Estonia, France, Germany**, Israel, Jamaica, Kenya, Korea, **Lithuania, Luxembourg**, Malaysia, Mexico, Montenegro, **Netherlands,** New Zealand, Norway, **Poland, Portugal**, Qatar, Singapore, **Spain, Sweden,** Tunisia, United Arab Emirates, United Kingdom, United States, Zambia	Kuwait, **Latvia**, Moldova, Saudi Arabia, Thailand	Georgia, Macedonia, Mauritius, Morocco, Oman, Rwanda, Serbia, Uruguay
Some DPE development (deviation from trend line is 5%–10%)	–	**Malta**	El Salvador, **Hungary,** Iceland, **Ireland**, Nepal, **Romania, Slovenia**	Japan, Namibia	–

(continued)

Table 5.1 (continued)

	Strong DE development (DE-EE difference is below −10%)	Some DE development (DE-EE difference is between −5% and 10%)	Keep balance between DE and EE (DE-EE difference is between −5% and 5%)	Some EE development (DE-EE difference is between 5% and 10%)	Strong EE development (DE-EE difference is above 10%)
Overall DPE development (deviation from trend line is over 10%)	Madagascar, Sri Lanka	**Austria,** Dominican Republic	Azerbaijan, Botswana, Burundi, Cambodia, Cameroon, **Cyprus**, Ethiopia, Guatemala, Hong Kong, Kazakhstan, Kyrgyzstan, Lebanon, Malawi, Mali, Nigeria, Panama, **Slovakia**, Taiwan, Turkey	Bangladesh, **Greece**, **Italy,** Mongolia, Paraguay, Russia	Algeria, Benin, Iran, Tanzania, Uganda, Zimbabwe

Note: *DE* digital ecosystem, *EE* entrepreneurship ecosystem; bold letters are the EU member countries

According to Fig. 5.4, a group consisting mainly of less developed countries have a positive deviation from the development implied trend line and a significantly higher digital ecosystem score than entrepreneurship ecosystem score (Quadrant I). For example, Morocco has a low DPE Index score, but it is higher than implied by its development. At the same time, the country's digital ecosystem score is much higher than the entrepreneurship ecosystem score. None of our examined countries belongs to this group.

A group of countries with a −5% to 5% range of difference between their digital ecosystem and entrepreneurship ecosystem scores that also have less than a −5% value in the DPE Index-DPE Index trend-line difference are considered optimal, which implies that no extra spending for DPE Index development is necessary and that their digital ecosystem-entrepreneurship ecosystem balance is more or less fine (Quadrant II). Germany, France, Poland, and Spain all belong to this group, together with many innovation-driven developed countries and some efficiency-driven developing countries. The United Kingdom, second in the DPE Index ranking, is also in this group. The positive 25% deviation from the implied development trend line suggests that the UK's digital entrepreneurship ecosystem is an important factor in its growth.

Quadrant III countries' overall DPE Index level is sufficient; however, their digital component is relatively underdeveloped in comparison to their entrepreneurship

Table 5.2 The DPE Index pillar scores of selected countries

Country/Pillar	France	Germany	Greece	Italy	Netherlands	Poland	United Kingdom
Digital access	82.8	82.0	41.2	50.6	84.0	49.1	96.7
Digital freedom	57.0	73.2	39.6	47.4	100.0	38.7	75.1
Digital protection	68.1	79.0	38.2	37.9	100.0	47.4	82.5
Digital literacy	56.1	87.7	27.7	45.1	**65.2**	34.4	95.2
Digital openness	69.0	73.1	38.4	37.6	80.5	49.5	85.5
Digital rights	61.2	68.4	39.0	57.2	78.6	52.3	68.2
Networking	**50.5**	**34.0**	24.9	**37.5**	95.4	**21.6**	91.8
Matchmaking	68.2	72.2	42.8	58.4	87.9	58.6	85.0
Financial facilitation	64.9	77.5	29.6	44.9	83.8	52.1	82.5
Digital adoption	71.6	75.0	60.7	58.7	75.1	43.2	84.4
Technology absorption	67.7	61.6	**24.6**	38.2	90.4	32.5	**73.9**
Technology transfer	61.0	69.4	38.3	47.9	74.5	38.5	89.0

Note: Bold letters are the weakest pillar values

component. China is in this group. Its DPE Index score is higher than implied by the trend line, but its entrepreneurship ecosystem score is higher than its digital ecosystem score (by 11.3%). Consequently, we recommend that China further efforts to improve its digital ecosystem.

Quadrant IV includes nations that spend too little on DPE Index development and their digital ecosystem is also less developed than their entrepreneurship ecosystem. Only four countries, including EU member Austria, are in this quadrant.

Quadrant V countries include those whose digital entrepreneurship ecosystem is significantly lower than that of similarly developed countries but their digital ecosystem and entrepreneurship ecosystem component development are within the acceptable range. EU members Hungary, Romania, Slovakia, and Slovenia belong to this group (Table 5.2).

Many countries have lower DPE Index scores than implied by the trend line and have imbalances in the digital ecosystem-entrepreneurship ecosystem context that favor digital ecosystem development (Quadrant VI). Note that we maximized the deviation at −35% in Fig. 5.4. Our highlighted examples are Italy and Greece, whose overall DPE Index development is well below what we would expect from developed countries. Moreover, their digital ecosystem component is more advanced than their entrepreneurship ecosystem component.

Table 5.1 provides further details about policy suggestions in terms of the DEE and the digital ecosystem and entrepreneurship ecosystem balance, based on Table 5.3 data. The recommendations are based on the deviation from the DPE Index trend line and the difference between the digital ecosystem and entrepreneurship ecosystem scores. As is clearly seen, most countries (41) and most EU member

Table 5.3 Digital platform economy optimization analysis for selected European countries: The distribution of additional resources for a 10% increase of the DPE Index scores

Country/Pillar	France	Germany	Greece	Italy	Netherlands	Poland	United Kingdom
Digital access	0%	0%	0%	0%	5%	0%	0%
Digital freedom	19%	0%	0%	2%	0%	0%	18%
Digital protection	2%	0%	0%	20%	0%	0%	9%
Digital literacy	19%	0%	21%	6%	31%	16%	0%
Digital openness	0%	0%	0%	22%	11%	0%	5%
Digital rights	11%	0%	0%	0%	12%	0%	27%
Networking	29%	100%	29%	22%	0%	64%	0%
Matchmaking	0%	0%	0%	0%	0%	0%	6%
Financial facilitation	6%	0%	18%	6%	5%	0%	9%
Digital adoption	0%	0%	0%	0%	17%	0%	6%
Technology absorption	2%	0%	32%	20%	0%	20%	20%
Technology transfer	13%	0%	0%	0%	19%	0%	1%
	100%	100%	100%	100%	100%	100%	100%

countries (15) are in the balanced category. Their DEE development should be in keeping with their balance between the digital ecosystem and entrepreneurship ecosystem. The second largest group (19) includes two EU member countries. Their digital ecosystem and entrepreneurship ecosystems are balanced, but these countries are well below the implied development trend line. Eleven countries belong to the cohort where the DEE level fits the level of development but the digital ecosystem requires significant improvement. Eight countries have a proper DEE level but poorly developed entrepreneurship ecosystems. Seven countries have DPE Index scores somewhat below the trend line and their digital ecosystem and entrepreneurship ecosystem are in balance. Four EU member countries are in this group. All the other groups contain fewer than seven countries. Note that only five EU member countries—Austria, Cyprus, Greece, Italy, and Slovakia—require substantial DEE development. It is also important to add that the trend line is an average performance. Therefore, if the EU wants to step ahead in the digital entrepreneurship ecosystem, the proper benchmarks are the USA, the United Kingdom, and The Netherlands.

5.3 The Increase of the DPE Index Scores: Optimizing Additional Resources

The distinctive methodological features of the DPE Index are designed to capture the unique characteristics of digital platform economy ecosystems, and thus to facilitate effective policymaking for these ecosystems. It captures the digital platform ecosystem dynamic by interacting with the digital and the entrepreneurship ecosystem components. It uses 12 interacted measures that are organized into four subindices. Importantly, it uses a PFB algorithm to facilitate the identification of bottleneck factors that hold back digital platform economy performance. See Appendix B for a detailed description of the DPE Index method.

The DPE Index methodology captures two important aspects that define the digital platform economy. First, it recognizes that the different pillars need to work together to create a high-quality ecosystem dynamic. Traditional indices fail to capture this aspect. In traditional indexing methods, the different components (pillars) are allowed to substitute for one another. In other words, a traditional index would allow, say, digital access to compensate for digital literacy. The DPE Index methodology requires that a high-quality digital platform economy dynamic has both digital access and high-quality digital literacy, in addition to the system's 10 other pillars. If one or more pillars perform poorly, it is likely to hold back the performance of the entire system. Although one can compensate to some degree for, say, digital access with digital literacy, the digital platform economy ecosystem is likely to grind to a halt if either element is completely absent.

The notion of bottlenecks derives directly from the notion that ecosystem elements interact to co-produce ecosystem performance. Because one cannot fully substitute individual pillars for others, poorly performing pillars can create bottlenecks that prevent the ecosystem from fully leveraging its strengths. To simulate this effect, the DPE Index methodology applies the PFB algorithm. This algorithm systematically penalizes ecosystem pillars according to its poorly performing pillars. By highlighting potential constraining factors in the entrepreneurial ecosystem, the PFB algorithm guides policy attention to the aspects of the ecosystem that may benefit most from coordinated policy action. These methodological innovations of the DPE Index provide important insights into the workings of digital platform economy ecosystems. Essential to the bottlenecks notion is that some factors may unduly constrain system performance beyond their objective importance. With the PFB methodology, it is possible to identify both where bottlenecks might lurk in any given system and how much the system performance will suffer as a result.

Table 5.2 presents the 12 pillar scores of selected European countries. It is clear that countries differ in the pillar configuration. While four countries—France, Germany, Italy, and Poland—have the same weakest pillar, networking, the size of the bottleneck is different in each case. The balance of the configuration also varies considerably. The difference between the lowest and the highest pillar values is around 23% in the well-balanced United Kingdom; in Germany it is more than 58%. Of the seven countries, Poland has the largest imbalance, followed by Greece and Germany. France, Italy, and The Netherlands are relatively well balanced; the difference between their lowest and the highest pillar scores is five percentage points (34% and 39%).

This basic analysis can be taken further. Because the DPE Index methodology allows the ecosystem pillars to interact, it is possible to conduct sensitivity analyses and simulate different policy scenarios. We present a case where additional policy efforts were taken in order to achieve a 10% increase in the overall DPE Index score. This analysis, presented in Table 5.3, shows how the additional policy efforts should be allocated across the 12 pillars, assuming equal cost to increase pillar performance. These figures were calculated by focusing policy efforts on the most pressing bottleneck until it was alleviated, then moving to the next most pressing bottleneck, and so on. The colors in Fig. 5.4 represent the severity of the bottleneck pillar: darker colors mean an effect that is more pervasive, while lighter colors mean less bottleneck influence.

The optimal policy mix—the targeted pillars and the assigned resources—is different in every case underlying the validity of the tailor-made, country-specific policy recommendations. France has a relatively well-balanced ecosystem where eight out of the 12 pillars need to improve to reach the desired 10% increase in the DPE Index score. France should spend 29% of the additional resources for the network pillar, 19% for digital freedom and digital literacy, 13% on technology transfer, and 11% on digital rights. Less than 10% is necessary to increase financial facilitation (6%), digital protection (2%), and technology absorption (2%). Similarly, The Netherlands should improve seven pillars, but its pillar composition differs from France. While Greece and Italy both have the same bottleneck as France and Poland, the share of the additional resources to ease the bottleneck effect is different in each case. Germany's one serious bottleneck is networking, thus it should focus all additional resources on improving this pillar. Poland also should spend the most to improve its network pillar, but its policymakers should also target digital absorption and digital literacy. The United Kingdom, second in the DPE Index ranking, has a very well-balanced ecosystem and should develop nine pillars in parallel. Unlike many EU member countries, the UK's networking pillar is fine; digital rights seem to be the most problematic.

While this simulation exercise obviously includes a number of simplifying assumptions (notably, equal cost to address each pillar; an equally applied bottleneck penalty for all pillars; pillars' equal ability to be changed by policy action), it nevertheless demonstrates the DPE Index methodology's ability to assess different policy scenarios. Although the scenarios should not be taken as prescriptive, the exercise nevertheless highlights priority areas that could be explored further. Another important benefit is that even this simplifying analysis suggests that there may be important differences among European countries in terms of policy priorities in facilitating the digital platform economy ecosystems.

5.4 The Full Profile of a Country: The Case of the United Kingdom

We benchmark the UK against Germany, as seen in Fig. 5.4. The UK is in line with Germany on the optimal balance between the digital and entrepreneurial ecosystems. However, the UK is much further along in its level of development, as seen in

Table 5.4 Digital platform economy profile of the United Kingdom

United Kingdom	Leaders
Digital platform economy index rank (score)	2 (82.7)
Digital technology infrastructure sub-index rank (score)	4 (83.1)
Digital user citizenship sub-index rank (score)	1 (81.4)
Digital multi-sided platform sub-index rank (score)	3 (84.4)
Digital technology entrepreneurship sub-index rank (score)	3 (81.3)

Pillars/Sub-Indices		Pillar/ sub-index score	Entrepreneurship ecosystem score	Digital ecosystem score
DTI	Digital access	96,7	92,9	82,9
	Digital freedom	75,1	77,4	80,2
	Digital protection	82,5	88,7	88,6
Digital technology infrastructure		83,1		
DUC	Digital literacy	95,2	76,2	88,6
	Digital openness	85,5	91,6	92,5
	Digital rights	68,2	92,1	58,8
Digital user citizenship		81,4		
DMP	Networking	91,8	100,0	85,6
	Matchmaking	85,0	91,0	91,0
	Financial facilitation	82,5	81,8	89,9
Digital multi-sided platform		84,8		
DTE	Digital adoption	84,4	83,9	77,7
	Technology absorption	73,9	78,4	84,7
	Technology transfer	89,0	95,1	85,2
Digital technology entrepreneurship		81,3		
Digital platform economy index		82,7	86,8	85,2

the trend line. What does this mean for its development strategy and what does it mean for policy?

We have developed presentation tools that are appropriate for examining the full profile of a country, up to the variable level. Our selected country is the UK, which is second in the DPE Index ranking, first in DUC, third in DMP and DTE, and fourth in DTI (Table 5.4). Here, we present the pillar values for each of the 12 DPE Index pillars. We also list the entrepreneurship ecosystem and digital ecosystem

Table 5.5 United Kingdom's policy optimization simulation: The allocation of additional resources among the pillars to reach a 10% increase in DPE Index score

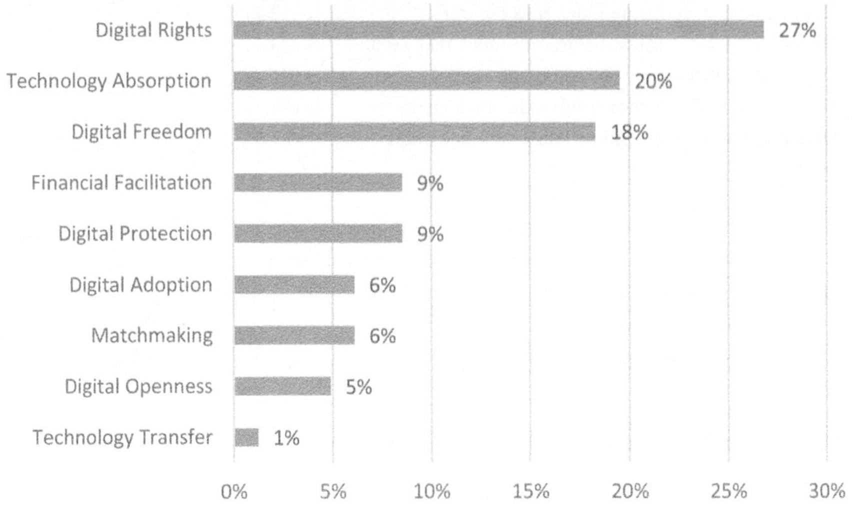

Note: Sum of additional resources for 10% DPE Index score increase (in unit per population) 82.0

component values. It is important to recognize that the scores of individual pillar components are NOT the result of simply multiplying the entrepreneurship and digital components. The DPE Index pillar scores are calculated from raw values. In the entrepreneurship ecosystem and digital ecosystem columns we report normalized and average adjusted values for the respective pillar components. The colors in each cell of the table denote the quartile in which the country is grouped for each component. A dark blue cell indicates the top quartile, light blue the second quartile. As we can see, the UK belongs to the top quartile in all but one aspect, the digital component of the digital rights pillar (Table 5.5).

Are the digital rights in the UK's digital ecosystem being held back by the EU? The defining issue confronting the EU for the past 3 years has been Brexit: the UK's departure from the EU after 40 years. Why the UK decided to leave the EU has been studied extensively by different scholars, who have looked at immigration, dysfunctional economics, regulations, rule of law, and cultural differences. We can identify three major areas of concern: economics, sovereignty, and culture.

The economic concerns have been partly about the EU as a dysfunctional economic entity. Policies on innovation, entrepreneurship, trade, and employment have led to large disparities in Europe between the rich north and the much poorer south. Staying in the EU would have pulled the UK down to the European level, and the UK would not have been able to realize its economic potential within the dysfunctional EU bureaucracy. According to Gramm and Toomey (2020), "Britain is leaving the European Union, which has trampled on British sovereignty, to escape its crippling regulatory structure" (p. 2). The second issue was the rise of nationalism

Table 5.6 The four sub-indices of selected EU countries, the UK, and the US

	Digital infrastucture governance	Digital citizenship	Digital platform	Digital technology entrepreneurship
France	63,5	64,9	60,3	65,3
Germany	67,6	70,3	**56,3**	**63,1**
Italy	40,7	50,3	**46,1**	**47,3**
Spain	54,0	53,1	52,5	53,7
United Kingdom	**80,1**	83,5	84,8	**81,3**
United States	**80,7**	79,0	87,4	**92,2**

around the world and the distrust of international organizations' ability to deal with global problems like security, trade, finance, inequality, and immigration. The sovereignty issue revolves around questions of whose rules countries will have to live under, an international organization like the EU or national rules set by each country. With the EU tightening its grip on its member states, the UK had limited freedom to enact its own laws and regulations. The final issue, culture, revolves around national identity and nationalism. These include but are not limited to issues of immigration and the impact of immigration and religion on cultural identity. Young people that voted against Brexit were influenced by cultural diversity and being a full-time student. No relationship was found with education (Ehsan & Sloam, 2020).

This leaves the question, why did Britain vote for Brexit? In an individual-level analysis Clarke et al. (2017) found that the economic influence and immigration-terrorism cost-benefit factors played a significant role in the vote to leave the EU. However, what has not been carefully researched is what aspect of the economic influence was most important to leaving? Was it innovation, technology, entrepreneurship, type of industry, or human capital? What the DPE Index shows is that the UK has a rather strong twenty-first-century digital entrepreneurial ecosystem but was stuck in a dysfunctional twentieth-century EU bureaucracy. If one looks at the simple scores of the four determinants of the DPE Index, we see that the United Kingdom is almost identical to the USA (Table 5.6). In other words, the four determinants are almost identical. Germany, Italy, and France lag way behind. If we look at the four determinants, the biggest differences are in agency. One interpretation of this is that the United Kingdom has a very strong DEE that was embedded in the rulemaking structure of the EU, which is itself emended into a twentieth-century version of the twenty-first century. To realize its economic potential, the UK had to extricate itself from the EU. London is the home of the largest knowledge base in the world: it hosts six of the top twenty universities in the world, the largest financial center in the world (along with New York City), and an increasingly entrepreneurial hub populated with global human capital. Therefore, the formation of the UK economy has been freed to focus on the twenty-first-century economy.

Germany is a different story. While the UK is a leader in digital entrepreneurship, Germany is a follower. This weaker position is holding Germany back from fully embracing a digital future. For example, as the engine of Europe, Germany's lack of startups has hindered it, especially in the area of information and digital technologies. The auto industry is a clear example: existing firms will not introduce new technologies, and Tesla's entry into Berlin (the information capital of Europe) is a shot across the bow of the European auto empire.

The German auto industry dominates the world in many respects, from the mass market to the luxury market and even the racing world. If we apply the Jovanovic analysis to the German auto industry, we can see why the industry would and would not implement new technologies. It would focus on product improvement that would produce cars that were over engineered. Hobijn and Jovanovic (2001) suggested that existing firms will not implement new technologies because of a lack of awareness and skill, vintage capital, and vested interests. The German auto industry fits this analysis like a glove. The industry has a huge investment in skills in the metal industry, engine transmissions, suspensions, and steering but a shortage of computer skills. The huge investment in vintage capital prevents it from easily writing off this investment. Finally, the heavy investment in governance of codetermination between labor, business, and government work councils makes meaningful restructuring almost impossible. This is reinforced by the top-down rules of the European Union.

Tesla's move to Berlin, the digital capital of Europe, is an indication that the future of the European auto industry may be with the startup and not the incumbent. Electric cars and self-driving vehicles are already here; however, they are not necessary evenly distributed. But, the direction of change is clear and the only unknown is the rate of change. However, once resource allocation decisions are redirected away from mechanical and diesel vehicles and toward electric vehicles, which are cleaner and in alignment with the issue of climate change, the rate of change could accelerate very quickly (Monsellato, 2016).

A deeper analysis of Tesla's global growth provides greater insight into the specific advantages of the company's business model, why entrepreneurs like Elon Musk chose to incorporate in the US, and what obstacles stand in the way of German innovation and entrepreneurship. Tesla serves as an unprecedented case study because "different government regulations have made entrance to the sector harder, since there are different standards in safety, emissions and standards. Recent history has showed that, besides Tesla Motors, no new player has entered the automotive industry in a significant manner in the last decades" (Monsellato, 2016, pp. 28–29). Indeed, the company has achieved what few previously thought was possible—it has turned a profit on a premium-priced electric vehicle with a developing supply chain that could bring affordable and sustainable high-tech cars to the middle class. If successful, such a profitable tech-driven business model would create a domino effect in innovation at Musk's other companies, SpaceX and SolarCity. Naturally, Tesla has utilized unconventional marketing to build the brand—a passion for transportation efficiency, high-tech adoption, and a sustainable footprint—and it has been noticed. The Tesla Model S has "earned numerous prizes like the Motor Trend Car of the Year 2013 and the World Green Car of the Year 2013" (Monsellato, 2016, pp. 86–87) and has chipped away at the German luxury automakers' market share. The great minds at Tesla fully embodied Schumpeterian entrepreneurship by identifying a need for electric vehicles in the market, foreseeing the demand desire and supply requirements, orchestrating a network of individuals with the knowledge and funds to create the new technology, and establishing strategic agreements with partners that could help scale commercialization and diversify their output in the long run. Because of Tesla's high degree of vertical integration, location in Silicon Valley, position as the sole automaker in the western US, and exceptional human capital (in addition to Musk's own credentials, he employs workers with backgrounds at Ford, Cisco, Apple, Oracle, GM, and German automakers), the startup went from a niche concept shop to a global player with a successfully sustained stock (Monsellato, 2016).[3]

[3] I would like to thank Mathew Boyer for these insights about Tesla.

Chapter 6
Summary and Conclusion

The recent digital and information-technology revolution has had a major impact on entrepreneurship. Platform-based developments in particular have helped to drastically reduce transaction costs and increase the appearance of new business models. This Schumpeterian type of organizational innovation has given birth to trillion dollar businesses like Apple, Alphabet, Amazon, Microsoft, and Facebook. These platforms and others provide a fertile field for Kirznerian-style digital entrepreneurs. However, digital entrepreneurs require a different environmental context than non-digital ones. Even if a country builds out its digital ecosystem, there is no guarantee it will be implemented by existing firms. In the same vein, if a country builds out its entrepreneurial ecosystem, there is no guarantee that startups will introduce new technologies. For technology to be introduced successfully, the digital ecosystem and the entrepreneurial ecosystem must be developed simultaneously. The digital entrepreneurship ecosystem theory developed by Sussan and Acs (2017) and amended by Song (2019) integrates the entrepreneurship ecosystem and the digital ecosystem concepts.

This paper builds on the DEE concept and provides a measurement of it. The DPE Index consists of four sub-indices (i.e., Digital User Citizenship, Digital Technology Infrastructure, Digital Multi-sided Platforms, and Digital Technology Entrepreneurship), 12 pillars (i.e., Digital Access, Digital Freedom, Digital Protection, Digital Literacy, Digital Openness, Digital Rights, Networking, Matchmaking, Financial Facilitation, Digital Adoption, Technology Absorption, and Technology Transfer), and 61 indices.

On a global scale, developed Anglo-Saxon and Nordic nations lead the DPE Index ranking, followed by other prosperous countries in Europe, Asia, and Oceania (i.e., Australia and New Zealand). Many mid-developed countries in Europe, Asia, and Latin America, together with some oil-rich countries (i.e., Bahrain, Oman, Qatar, Saudi Arabia, and United Arab Emirates) report below-average DPE Index scores. In terms of the DPE Index, the poorly performing countries include underdeveloped African and Asian countries, as well as some developing European and

L. Szerb et al., *The Digital Platform Economy Index 2020*, SpringerBriefs in Economics, https://doi.org/10.1007/978-3-030-89651-5_6

Latin American nations. The specific analysis for the EU reveals that most countries (22 out of 27) are on or above the implied development trend line; however, they are far from the DPE Index's two top-performing countries (the US and UK), with the exception of The Netherlands. The gap between the US and the large EU member countries like Germany and France is significant, around 25%. Spain, Italy, and Poland lag behind the US by more than 35%. The EU platformization lag stems from the fact that incumbent firms in Europe have not introduced new technologies in sufficient volume, and startups have remained small and not scalable (Naudé, 2016). It seems that the EU's institutional setup is better suited to the self-employment type of small business than to fast growing billion-dollar businesses, the unicorns. If the EU is to survive and prosper, it must rebalance its digital entrepreneurial ecosystem policies to promote technology innovation and platform companies, and create a sustainable platform economy.

The Applied Indicators in the Digital Entrepreneurship Index

In the following Tables A.1, A.2, A.3 and A.4—we describe all the applied indicators in the DPE Index. The four tables represent the four sub-indices of the DPE Index.

The first column of the tables represents the abbreviated name of the particular indicator. It consists of three parts. The first part is always the name of the sub-index, the second is the number of the pillar, and the third is the number of the indicator. The indicators belonging to a particular pillar are denoted by different colors.

The second column contains the full name of the indicator, the source of the data, and the year of the survey. The bottom part of the second column cell incudes the full name of the pillar and the type of indicator. There are four types of indicators: Institutions and Agent are part of the entrepreneurship ecosystem, and Digital Technology and Users are part of the digital ecosystem.

The third column contains the full description of the particular indicator.

L. Szerb et al., *The Digital Platform Economy Index 2020*, SpringerBriefs in Economics, https://doi.org/10.1007/978-3-030-89651-5

Table A.1 The applied indicators of the DTI sub-index

DUC_ P2_I1	*Fixed broadband internet subscriptions/100 pop.* Global Competitiveness Index, 2017–2018 (2016 or most recent data) Digital access - Users	Fixed-broadband internet subscriptions per 100 population
	Int'l internet bandwidth, kb/s per user Global Competitiveness Index, 2017–2018 (2016 data) Digital access - Users	International internet bandwidth (kb/s) per internet user
DUC_ P2_I2	*Percentage of households equipped with a personal computer* World Telecommunication/ICT Indicators Database, 4 January 2018 (2017 data) Digital access - users	Percentage of households equipped with a personal computer
	Percentage of individuals using a computer World Telecommunication/ICT Indicators Database, 4 January 2018 (2017 data) Digital access - users	Percentage of individuals using a computer
DUC_ P2_I3	*Global cybersecurity index technical sub-index* ITU, 2017 Digital access - institution	Technical: Measured based on the existence of technical institutions and frameworks dealing with cybersecurity
DUC_ P2_I4	*Global cybersecurity index technical sub-index* ITU, 2017 Digital access - institution	Organizational: Measured based on the existence of policy coordination institutions and strategies for cybersecurity development at the national level
DIG_ P2_I1	*Business freedom* Index of Economic Freedom, 2018 (data 2016, 2017) Digital freedom - institutions	Business freedom is an overall indicator of the efficiency of government regulation of business. The quantitative score is derived from an array of measurements of the difficulty of starting, operating, and closing a business
DIG_ P2_I2	*Freedom of the press* Freedom House, 2017 (data 2016) Digital freedom - institutions	Annual report on media independence around the world, assesses the degree of print, broadcast, and digital media freedom in 199 countries and territories
	Freedom in the world Freedom House, 2018 (data 2017) Digital freedom - institutions	Freedom in the World is an annual global report on political rights and civil liberties, composed of numerical ratings and descriptive texts for each country and a select group of territories. The 2018 edition covers developments in 195 countries and 14 territories from January 1, 2017, through December 31, 2017. It uses a three-tiered system consisting of scores, ratings, and status. The complete list of the questions used in the scoring process, and the tables for converting scores to ratings and ratings to status, appear at the end of this essay

(continued)

Table A.1 (continued)

DIG_ P2_I3	*Internet & telephony competition/ global Cyberlaw tracker* ICT Regulatory Tracker, ITU, 2017 Digital freedom - digital technology	Competition framework for the ICT sector (level of competition in the main market segments)
DIG_ P2_I4	*Generic top-level domains (gTLDs)* Global Innovation Index, 2017 (data 2016) Digital freedom - digital technology	Generic top-level domains (gTLDs) (per thousand population 15–69 years old)
	Internet domains/1000 population Webhosting, 2015 Digital freedom - digital technology	Number of active internet domain registrations per 1000 number of population
DIG_ P3_I1	*Software piracy rate, % software installed* WEF Network Readiness Index, 2013 data Digital protection - digital technology	Unlicensed software units as a percentage of total software units installed. This measure covers piracy of all packaged software that runs on personal computers (PCs), including desktops, laptops, and ultra-portables, including netbooks. This includes operating systems; systems software such as databases and security packages; business applications; and consumer applications such as games, personal finance, and reference software. The study does not include software that runs on servers or mainframes, or software loaded onto tablets or smart phones
DIG_ P3_I2	*Secure internet servers/million pop.* WEF Network Readiness Index 2016 report (2014 data) Digital protection - digital technology	Secure internet servers per million population
DIG_ P3_I3	*Corruption perception index* Corruption perception index (CPI), 2017 (data 2016–2018) Digital protection - institutions	The index, which ranks 180 countries and territories by their perceived levels of public sector corruption according to experts and businesspeople, uses a scale of 0 to 100, where 0 is highly corrupt and 100 is very clean
DIG_ P3_I4	*Global cybersecurity index legal sub-index (GCI), 2017* Digital protection - institutions	The GCI revolves around the ITU global cybersecurity agenda (GCA) and its five pillars (legal, technical, organizational, capacity building. And cooperation). For each of these pillars, questions were developed to assess commitment. Legal component is based on the existence of legal institutions and frameworks dealing with cybersecurity and cybercrime

Table A.2 The applied indicators of the DUC sub-index

DUC_ P1_I1	*Digital skills among population* Global Competitiveness Index, 2017, WEF Digital literacy – Users	Executive Opinion Survey: "In your country, to what extent does the active population possess sufficient digital skills (e.g., computer skills, basic coding, digital reading)? (1 = not at all, 7 = to a great extent)"
DUC_ P1_I2	*Number of searches by users in a country* The Digital Country Index, 2017 Digital literacy - users	First presented in 2015, the digital country index tracks the number of searches performed by all worldwide citizens toward any given country, in connection with six topic areas: Tourism, investment, exports, talent, and national prominence
DUC_ P1_I3	*Quality of the education system,* 1–7 (*best*) Global Competitiveness Index, 2017–2018 (data 2015–2016 average) Digital literacy - institutions	In your country, how well does the education system meet the needs of a competitive economy? [1 = not well at all; 7 = extremely well]
DUC_ P1_I4	*Internet access in schools,* 1–7 (*best*) Global Competitiveness Index, 2017–2018 (data 2015–2016 average) Digital literacy - institutions	In your country, to what extent is the internet used in schools for learning purposes? [1 = not at all; 7 = to a great extent]
DIG_ P1_I1	*Laws relating to ICTs,* 1–7 (*best*) World Economic Forum, Executive Opinion Survey, 2014 and 2015 editions Digital openness - institutions	How developed are your country's laws relating to the use of ICTs (e.g., e-commerce, digital signatures, consumer protection)? [1 = not developed at all; 7 = extremely well developed]
DIG_ P1_I2	*Global Cyberlaw tracker* UNCTAD, 19/12/2017 Digital openness - institutions	Tracks the state of e-commerce legislation in the field of e-transactions, consumer protection, data protection/privacy, and cybercrime adoption in the 194 UNCTAD member states. It indicates whether or not a given country has adopted legislation, or has a draft law pending adoption. In some instances where information about a country's legislation adoption was not readily available, "no data" is indicated.
DIG_ P1_I3	*Percentage of individuals using the internet* World Telecommunication/ICT Indicators Database, 2018 (2016 data) Digital openness - digital technology	Percentage of individuals using the internet
DIG_ P1_I4	*Percentage of households with internet access at home* World Telecommunication/ICT Indicators Database, 2018 (2017 data) Digital openness - digital technology	Percentage of households with internet access at home
DUC_ P3_I1	*Net infection ratio* Securelist statistics, Kaspersky, download: 17/03/2018 (monthly data) Digital rights - users	The map shows the percentages of users on whose devices Kaspersky lab products intercepted local infections in the last 24 hours. KL products' users are always protected from all—Even the very latest—Threats.

(continued)

Table A.2 (continued)

DUC_ P3_I2	*Internet censorship and surveillance* Wikipedia, 2018 Digital rights - users	Detailed country by country information on internet censorship and surveillance is provided in the freedom on the net reports from freedom house, by the OpenNet initiative, by reporters without Borders, and in the country reports on human rights practices from the U.S. State Department Bureau of democracy, human rights, and labor. The ratings produced by several of these organizations are summarized below, as well as in the censorship by country article. Four category rating: 1: Pervasive; 2: Selective; 3: Substantial; 4: Little or none
DUC_ P3_I3	*Personal rights* The Global Talent Competitiveness Report, 2018 (2016 data) Digital rights - institution	Personal rights are a component in the opportunity dimension of the social Progress index. This component is based on five variables: Political rights, freedom of speech, freedom of assembly/ association, freedom of movement, and private property rights.
	Fundamental rights Rule of Law Index, World Justice Project, 2017–2018 Digital rights - institution	Equal treatment and absence of discrimination 4.2 the right to life and security of the person is effectively guaranteed 4.3 due process of law and rights of the accused 4.4 freedom of opinion and expression is effectively guaranteed 4.5 freedom of belief and religion is effectively guaranteed 4.6 freedom from arbitrary interference with privacy is effectively guaranteed 4.7 freedom of assembly and association is effectively guaranteed 4.8 fundamental labor rights are effectively guaranteed
	Property rights International Property Rights Index, Property Rights Alliance, 2013 Digital rights - institution	The average of the two sub-indices as physical property rights and intellectual property rights from international property rights index

Table A.3 The applied indicators of the DMSP sub-index

DMSP_ P1_I1	*Use of virtual social networks,* 1–7 (*best*) WEF Network Readiness Index, 2016 (2014–2015 average data) Networking - users	In your country, how widely are virtual social networks used (e.g., Facebook, twitter, LinkedIn)? [1 = not at all used; 7 = used extensively]
DMSP_ P1_I2	*Social media penetration* 2017 digital yearbook internet, social media, and mobile data Networking - users	Active social media users, penetration (%)
DMSP_ P1_I3	*Use of virtual professional networks* The Global Talent Competitiveness Report, 2018 (2015 data) Networking - users	LinkedIn users refers to the number of registered LinkedIn accounts per 1000 labor force (15–64 years old)
DMSP_ P1_I4	*ICT use for business-to-business transactions,* 1–7 (*best*) WEF Network Readiness Index, 2016 (2014–2015 average data) Networking - agent	In your country, to what extent do businesses use ICTs for transactions with other businesses? [1 = not at all; 7 = to a great extent]
DMSP_ P1_I5	*Business-to-consumer internet use,* 1–7 (*best*) WEF Network Readiness Index, 2016 (2014–2015 average data) Networking - agent	In your country, to what extent do businesses use the internet for selling their goods and services to consumers? [1 = not at all; 7 = to a great extent]
DMSP_ P2_I1	*Wikipedia yearly edits* Global Innovation Index, 2017 (2016 data) Matchmaking - users	Wikipedia yearly edits by country (per million population 15–69 years old). 2014data extracted from Wikimedia Foundation's internal data sources. For every country with more than 100,000 edit counts in 2016, the data from 2016 are used. For all other countries, the data from 2014 are utilized. The data excludes bot contributions to the extent that is identifiable in the data sources. Data are reported per million population 15–69 years old.
DMSP_ P2_I2	*Video uploads on YouTube* Global Innovation Index, 2017, (2016 data) Matchmaking - users	Number of video uploads on YouTube (scaled by population 15–69 years old) | 2015Total number of video uploads on YouTube, per country, scaled by population15–69 years old. The raw data are survey based: The country of affiliation is chosen by each user on the basis of a multi-choice selection. This metric counts all video upload events by users. For confidentiality reasons, only normalized values are reported; while relative positions are preserved, magnitudes are not
DMSP_ P2_I3	*Number of professional developers/ population* *Developer Survey Results, 2017 (2016 data)* Matchmaking - agent	Ratio of professional developers

(continued)

Table A.3 (continued)

DMSP_ P3_I1	*Credit card* (*% age* 15+) World Bank Global Financial Inclusion, 2017 Financial facilitation - users	Denotes the percentage of respondents who report having a credit card (% age 15+). [ts: Data are available for multiple waves].
	Debit card (*% age* 15+) World Bank Global Financial Inclusion, 2017 Financial facilitation - users	Denotes the percentage of respondents who report having a debit card (% age 15+). [ts: Data are available for multiple waves].
DMSP_ P3_I2	*Used the internet to pay bills or to buy something online in the past year* (*% age 15+*) World Bank Global Financial Inclusion, 2017 Financial facilitation - users	Denotes the percentage of respondents who report paying bills or making purchases online using the internet in the past 12 months (% age 15+). [w2: Data are available for wave 2].
DMSP_ P3_I3	*Used a mobile phone or the internet to access a financial institution account in the past year* (*% age* 15+) World Bank Global Financial Inclusion, 2017 Financial facilitation - users	Denotes the percentage of respondents who used a mobile phone or the internet to access a financial institution account in the past year (% with an account, age 15+). [w2: Data are available for wave 2].
DMSP_ P3_I4	*Made or received digital payments in the past year* (*% age* 15+) Financial facilitation - users	Denotes the percentage of respondents who report making or receiving digital payments in the past 12 months (% age 15+).
DMSP_ P3_I5	*Depth of Capital Market Sub-Index Score* (*US* 2016 = 100) World Bank Global Financial Inclusion, 2017 (data 2016) Financial facilitation - agent	The depth of capital market is one of the six sub-indices of the venture capital and private equity index. This variable is a complex measure of the size and liquidity of the stock market, level of IPO, M&A, and debt and credit market activity.
DMSP_ P3_I6	*FinTech business* Dealroom, 26/03/2018 Financial facilitation - agent	The number of financial technology businesses standardized by the number of population (2018), own calculation
DMSP_ P3_I7	*Venture capital availability* Global Competitiveness Index, 2017–2018 (2016–2017 average data) Financial facilitation - agent	Answers to the question: In your country, how easy is it for entrepreneurs with innovative but risky projects to find venture capital? [1 = extremely difficult; 7 = extremely easy], (world economic forum dataset)

Table A.4 The applied indicators of DTE sub-index

DTE_ P1_I1	*Quality of electricity supply, 1–7 (best)* Global Competitiveness Index, 2017.2018 (2016–2017 average data) Digital adoption - digital technology	In your country, how reliable is the electricity supply (lack of interruptions and lack of voltage fluctuations)? [1 = extremely unreliable; 7 = extremely reliable]
	Electricity production, kWh/ capita WEF Network Readiness Index, 2016 (2013 data) Digital adoption - digital technology	Electricity production (kWh) per capita
DTE_ P1_I2	*Fixed telephone lines/100 pop.* Global Competitiveness Index, 2017.2018 (2016–2017 average data) Digital adoption - digital technology	Number of fixed-telephone lines per 100 population
DTE_ P1_I3	*Mobile telephone subscriptions/100 pop.** Global Competitiveness Index, 2017.2018 (2016–2017 average data) Digital adoption - digital technology	Number of mobile-cellular telephone subscriptions per 100 population
DTE_ P1_I4	*Mobile network coverage, % pop.* WEF Network Readiness Index, 2016 (2014 data) Digital adoption - digital technology	Percentage of total population covered by a mobile network signal
DTE_ P1_I5	*Computer software spending* Global Innovation Index, 2018(2016 data) Digital adoption - agent	Total computer software spending (% of GDP)
DTE_ P1_I6	*Skills of workforce* Global Innovation Index, 2018 Digital adoption - agent	Skills, a pillar of GCI, consist of two parts, skills of current workforce and skills of future workforce
DTE_ P2_I1	*Data centers* Data Centers Catalog, 2019 Technology absorption - digital technology	Combined data centers number and density based on population
DTE_ P2_I2	*Availability of latest technologies,* 1–7 (*best*) Global Competitiveness Index, 2017–2018 (2016–2017 average data) Digital technology absorption - Technology absorption - digital technology	In your country, to what extent are the latest technologies available? [1 = not at all; 7 = to a great extent]

(continued)

Table A.4 (continued)

DTE_ P2_I3	*Knowledge absorption (sub-index in GII)* Global Innovation Index, 2017 (data 2016) Digital technology absorption - Technology absorption - agent	It reveals how good economies are at absorbing knowledge. A complex variable from GII consisting of five indicators "..That are linked to sectors with high-tech content or are key to innovation: Royalty and license fees payments as a percentage of total trade; high-tech imports (net of re-imports) as a percentage of total imports; imports of communication, computer, and information services as a percentage of total trade; and net inflows of foreign direct investment (FDI) as a percentage of GDP. To strengthen the sub-pillar, the percentage of research talent in business was added this year to provide a measurement of professionals engaged in the conception or creation of new knowledge, products, processes, methods, and systems, including business management." (p. 54)
DTE_ P2_I4	*Impact of ICTs on business models,* 1–7 (*best*) Global Innovation Index, 2017 (2016 data) Technology absorption - agent	Average answer to the question: In your country, to what extent do ICTs enable new business models? [1 = not at all; 7 = to a great extent]
	Impact of ICTs on new organizational models, 1–7 (*best*) Global Innovation Index, 2017 (2016 data) Technology absorption - agent	Average answer to the question: In your country, to what extent do ICTs enable new organizational models?
DTE_ P3_I1	*Knowledge and technology outputs (GII)* The Global Innovation Index, 2017 (2016 data) Technology transfer - digital technology	A sub-index of GII consisting of three parts, knowledge creation, knowledge impact, and knowledge diffusion
DTE_ P1_I2	*Capacity for innovation* Global Competitiveness Index, 2007–2017 Technology transfer - digital technology	In your country, to what extent do companies have the capacity to innovate? [1 = not at all; 7 = to a great extent]
DTE_ P2_I3	*High-level skills (GTCI)* The Global Talent Competitiveness Report, 2018 (data 2015) Technology transfer - agent	The average of six indicators: Workforce with tertiary education, population with tertiary education, professionals, researchers, senior officials and managers, availability of scientists and engineers
DTE_ P2_I4	*Startups* Startup ranking, 2018 Technology transfer - agent	Number of startups, a normalized average of the population standardized startups and the log of startups in the country

Table A.4 (continued)

The Calculation of the DPE Index and the Components Scores

According to the model pictured in Fig. 1 and detailed in Fig. 2, we suggest a five-level composite indicator following as (1) indicators (2) variables, (3) pillars, (4) sub-indices, and (5) the super index. The super index is called the Digital Platform Economy Index and its sub-indices are the four frameworks. The 12 components are called pillars. Pillars are the most important constituents of the model. Pillars are comprised of 24 variables representing digital ecosystem (12) and entrepreneurship ecosystem (12). Variables are built from 61 indicators that are the elementary building blocks of the DPE Index

Indicator selection was based on three criteria:

1. Relevance of the indicator for the phenomenon we aim to measure.
2. Specificity of the variable to the phenomenon it represents.
3. Potentially flawless and clear interpretation of the indicator.

We also aimed to have the indicator available for at least 90% of the countries, but in five cases, we could not reach this goal. The indicators are available as follows: for 85 countries more than 95.1%, for 23 countries 90.1–95.0%, and for 8 countries 80.1–90.0%. The results for these eight countries—Benin, Burundi, Hong Kong, Jamaica, Macedonia, Madagascar, Namibia, Taiwan—should be viewed with caution. Variables were calculated from normalized indicator scores. Following the Global Entrepreneurship Index building methodology, we provide the most important steps of calculation (Acs et al. 2014).

All pillars contain two types of variables: one is representing the digital ecosystem (digital technology and users) and the other representing the entrepreneurship ecosystem (institutions and agents). The overall influence of these two types of variables is captured by multiplying the two components:

$$\text{DPE\_pillar}_{i,j} = \text{DE\_variable}_{i,j} * \text{EE\_variable}_{i,j} \tag{A.1}$$

L. Szerb et al., *The Digital Platform Economy Index 2020*, SpringerBriefs in Economics, https://doi.org/10.1007/978-3-030-89651-5

where.
$i = 1 \ldots n$, the number of countries
$DPE\_pillar_{i,j}$ represents the digital entrepreneurship ecosystem pillars, j = 1,….0.12.
$DE\_pillar_{i,j}$ represents the digital ecosystem pillars, j = 1,….0.12
$EE\_pillar_{i,j}$ represents the entrepreneurship ecosystem pillars, j = 1,….0.12

After the calculation of the raw pillar scores, we normalized them using the distance methodology:

$$\text{DPE\_pillar}(norm)_{i,j} = \frac{\text{DPE\_pillar}_{i,j}}{\max \text{DPE\_pillar}_{i,j}} \tag{A.2}$$

for all j = 1 … 12, the number of pillars.
where DPE _ pillar$(norm)_{i,k}$ is the normalized score value for country i and pillar j.
max DPE _ pillar $p_{i,j}$ is the maximum value for pillar j.

When we calculate the normalized averages of the 12 pillars for the 116 countries, it ranges from 0.153 (matchmaking) to 0.525 (digital rights) with 0.361 overall average value. The different averages of the normalized values of the pillars imply that reaching the same pillar values requires different efforts and resources. Consequently, the effect of additional resources to achieve the same marginal improvement of the pillar values is different and it is problematic in using the pillar values for public policy purposes. The average pillar adjustment methodology developed by Acs, Autio, and Szerb (2014) reduces but does not fully eliminate this problem.

The following Eqs. (A.3a), (A.3b), (A.3c) show the calculation steps.

First, we calculate the average value of the j = 12 pillar:

$$\overline{\text{DPE\_pillar}(norm)_{\text{j}}} = \frac{\sum_{\text{i=1}}^{\text{n}} \text{DPE\_pillar}(norm)_{\text{i,j}}}{\text{n}} \quad \text{for all j} \tag{A.3a}$$

where $\overline{\text{DPE\_pillar}(norm)_{\text{j}}}$ is the average value of all j = 12 normalized pillars.

We want to transform the DPE _ pillar$(norm)_{i,j}$ values such that the potential values to be in the [0,1] range.

$$DPE\text{\_pillar}(\text{equal})_{\text{i,j}} = \text{DPE\_pillar}(norm)_{\text{i,j}}^{\text{t}} \tag{A.3b}$$

where t is the “strength of adjustment,” the t-th moment of DEE _ pillar$(norm)_j$ is exactly the needed average, $\text{DPE\_pillar(equal)}_j$.

We have to find the root of the following equation for t:

$$\sum_{\text{i=1}}^{\text{n}} \text{DPE\_pillar}(norm)_{\text{I,j}}^{\text{t}} - \text{n}\overline{\text{DPE\_pillar}(\text{equal})_{\text{j}}} = 0 \tag{A.3c}$$

For the solution, the Newton–Raphson method is used with an initial guess of 0. After obtaining t, the computations are straightforward.

After these transformations, the Penalty for Bottleneck methodology was used to create pillar-adjusted PFB values. A bottleneck is defined as the worst performing pillar or a limiting constraint in a particular country's digital entrepreneurship system. Here, bottleneck is defined as the lowest level of a particular pillar, relative to other pillars in a particular country. This notion of a bottleneck is important for policy purposes considering the systemic nature of DEE. The system perspective means that that pillars have an effect on one another. This interaction should be included in the calculation of the pillar, the sub-index, and the DPE Index scores. We consider the system being optimal if all the average adjusted pillar scores are the same for the particular country. Differences imply non-optimal use of the resources. Practically, it means that after equalizing the pillar averages, the value of each pillar of a country is penalized by linking it to the score of the pillar with the weakest scores in that country. This simulates the notion of a bottleneck; if the weakest pillar was improved, the whole DPE Index would show a significant improvement.

We define our penalty function following as:

$$DPE\_penalized_{(i),j} = 100 * \min DPE\_pillar(equal)_{(i),j} + \left(1 - e^{-\left(y_{(i)j} - \min DPE\_pillar(equal)_{(i),j}\right)}\right) \tag{A.4}$$

where $DPE\_penalized_{i,j}$ is the modified, post-penalty value of pillar j in country i.
$DPE\_pillar(equal)_{i,j}$ is the normalized value of index component j in country i.
$DPE\_pillar(equal)_{min}$ is the lowest value of $y_{i,j}$ for country i.
i = 1, 2,......116 = the number of countries.
j = 1, 2,.......12 = the number of pillars.

Note, that the multiplication by 100 is purely practical to get a 0–100-point scale instead of the 0–1 range.

Sub-index calculation is simple, just taking the arithmetic average of its PFB-adjusted pillars for that sub-index:

$$DIG_i = \sum_{j=1}^{3} \frac{DPE\_penalized_j}{3} \tag{A.5a}$$

$$DUC_i = \sum_{j=4}^{6} \frac{DPE\_penalized_j}{3} \tag{A.5b}$$

$$DMSP_i = \sum_{j=7}^{9} \frac{DPE\_penalized_j}{3} \tag{A.5c}$$

$$\mathrm{DTE_i} = \sum_{j=10}^{12} \frac{\mathrm{DPE\_penalized_j}}{3} \tag{A.5d}$$

where DIG_i = Digital Technology Infrastructure score for country i,
DUC_i = Digital User Citizenship score for country i,
DMSP_i = Digital Multi-sided Platform score for country i, and,
DTE_i = Digital Technology Entrepreneurship score for country i.

Finally, the DPE Index score is calculated as the simple arithmetic average of the four sub-indices:

$$\mathrm{DPE}_i = \frac{1}{4}\left(DIG_i + DUC_i + DMSP_i + DTE_i\right) \tag{A.6}$$

where DPE_i is the Digital Platform Economy index score for country *i*.

We have done the basic tests for consistency of the composite indicator components. The Cronbach alpha values for the four sub-indices are in an acceptable range: for DUC = 0.93, for DTE = 0.84, for DMP = 0.92, and for DTE = 0.93.

References

Acs, Z. J., Autio, E., & Szerb, L. (2014). National systems of entrepreneurship: Measurement issues and policy implications. *Research Policy, 43*(3), 476–494. https://doi.org/10.1016/j.respol.2013.08.016

Alkire, L., Pohlmann, J., & Barnett, W. (2019). Triggers and motivators of privacy protection behavior on Facebook. *Journal of Services Marketing, 33*(1), 57–72.

Alt, R., Beck, R., & Smits, M. T. (2018). Fin tech and the transformation of the financial industry. *Electronic Markets, 28*(3), 235–243.

Amit, R., & Zott, C. (2012). Creating value through business model innovation. *MIT Sloan Management Review, 53*, 41–49.

Andrews, D., Criscuolo, C., & Gal, P. N. (2015). Frontier firms, technology diffusion and public policy. OECD Future of Productivity Background Paper. OECD Future of Productivity Background Paper.

Autio, E., Szerb, L., Komlosi, E., & Tiszberger, M. (2018). *The European index of digital entrepreneurship systems (JRC technical reports, 153)*. Publications Office of the European Union.

Autio, E., Szerb, L., Komlosi, E., & Tiszberger, M. (2019). EIDES 2019—The European index of digital entrepreneurship systems (No. JRC117495). Joint Research Centre.

Baierl, R., Behrens, J., & Brem, A. (2019). *Digital entrepreneurship*. Springer.

Baron, R. J. (2019). Digital literacy. In R. Hobbs & P. Mihailidis (Eds.), *The international encyclopedia of media literacy* (Vol. 2, pp. 343–349). Wiley Blackwell.

Batabyal, A. A., & Nijkamp, P. (2016). Digital technologies, knowledge spillovers, innovation policies, and economic growth in a creative region. *Economics of Innovation and New Technology, 25*(5), 470–484.

Becker, J., Knackstedt, R., & Pöppelbuß, J. (2009). Developing maturity models for IT management. *Business & Information Systems Engineering, 1*(3), 213–222.

Bélanger, F., & Crossler, R. E. (2011). Privacy in the digital age: A review of information privacy research in information systems. *MIS Quarterly, 35*(4), 1017–1042.

Berners-Lee, T. (2009). The next web. What's next in tech session: TED conference, Long Beach, CA. https://www.ted.com/talks/tim_berners_lee_on_the_next_web

Bock, W., Wilms, M., Soos, P., & Roeber, B. (2014). Reforming Europe's telecoms regulation to enable the digital single market. *Communications and Strategies, 93*, 17–34.

Buckingham, D. (2006). Defining digital literacy. *Digital Kompetanse, 1*(4), 263–276.

Cavallo, A., Ghezzi, A., & Balocco, R. (2018). Entrepreneurial ecosystem research: Present debates and future directions. *International Entrepreneurship and Management Journal, 15*, 1291–1321. https://doi.org/10.1007/s11365-018-0526-3

L. Szerb et al., *The Digital Platform Economy Index 2020*, SpringerBriefs in Economics, https://doi.org/10.1007/978-3-030-89651-5

Chaudhry, P. E., Chaudhry, S. S., Stumpf, S. A., & Sudler, H. (2011). Piracy in cyber space: Consumer complicity, pirates and enterprise enforcement. *Enterprise Information Systems, 5*(2), 255–271.

Chesbrough, H. (2006). *Open business models: How to thrive in the new innovation landscape*. Harvard Business School Press.

Christin, D., Reinhardt, A., Kanhere, S. S., & Hollick, M. (2011). A survey on privacy in mobile participatory sensing applications. *Journal of Systems and Software, 84*(11), 1928–1946.

Clarke, H. D., Goodwin, M., & Whiteley, P. (2017). Why Britain voted for Brexit: An individual-level analysis of the 2016 referendum vote. *Parliamentary Affairs, 70*(3), 439–464.

Cruz-Jesus, F., Oliveira, T., Bacao, F., & Irani, Z. (2017). Assessing the pattern between economic and digital development of countries. *Information Systems Frontiers, 19*(4), 835–854.

Cusumano, M. A., Gawer, A., & Yoffie, D. B. (2019). *The business of platforms: Strategy in the age of digital competition, innovation, and power*. HarperCollins.

Dede, C. (2010). Technological supports for acquiring 21st century skills. *International Encyclopedia of Education, 3*, 158–166.

Ehsan, R., & Sloam, J. (2020). Resources, values, identity: Young cosmopolitans and the referendum on British membership of the European Union. *Parliamentary Affairs, 73*(1), 46–65.

Elia, G., Margherita, A., & Passiante, G. (2020). Digital entrepreneurship ecosystem: How digital technologies and collective intelligence are reshaping the entrepreneurial process. *Technological Forecasting and Social Change, 150*, 119791.

Evans, D. S. (2013). Economics of vertical restraints for multi-sided platforms. University of Chicago Institute for Law & Economics Olin Research Paper, 626.

Evans, D. S., & Schmalensee, R. (2007). *Catalyst code: The strategies behind the world's most dynamic companies*. Harvard Business School Press.

Evans, D. S., & Schmalensee, R. (2016). *Matchmakers: The new economics of multi-sided platforms*. Harvard Business Review Press.

Farrell, J., & Klemperer, P. (2007). Coordination and lock-in: Competition with switching costs and network effects. *Handbook of Industrial Organization, 3*, 1967–2072.

Ferguson, N. (2019). *The square and the tower: Networks and power, from the freemasons to Facebook*. Penguin Books.

Fong, M. W. (2009). Digital divide: The case of developing countries. *Issues in Informing Science and Information Technology, 6*(2), 471–478.

Friemel, T. N. (2016). The digital divide has grown old: Determinants of a digital divide among seniors. *New Media & Society, 18*(2), 313–331.

Gawer, A. (Ed.). (2009). *Platforms, markets, and innovation*. Edward Elgar.

Gawer, A. (2014). Bridging differing perspectives on technological platforms: Toward an integrative framework. *Research Policy, 43*(7), 1239–1249.

Ghobadi, S., & Ghobadi, Z. (2015). How access gaps interact and shape digital divide: A cognitive investigation. *Behaviour & Information Technology, 34*(4), 330–340.

Goldfarb, A., & Tucker, C. (2019). Digital economics. *Journal of Economic Literature, 57*(1), 3–43.

Gomber, P., Kauffman, R. J., Parker, C., & Weber, B. W. (2018). On the FinTech revolution: Interpreting the forces of innovation, disruption, and transformation in financial services. *Journal of Management Information Systems, 35*(1), 220–265.

Gomber, P., Koch, J. A., & Siering, M. (2017). Digital finance and FinTech: Current research and future research directions. *Journal of Business Economics, 87*(5), 537–580.

Gompers, P., & Lerner, J. (2001). The venture capital revolution. *Journal of Economic Perspectives, 15*(2), 145–168.

Goodfellow, R. (2011). Literacy, literacies and the digital in higher education. *Teaching in Higher Education, 16*(1), 131–144. https://doi.org/10.1080/13562517.2011.54412

Gramm, P., & Toomey, P. (2020). U.S. and U.K. can set a standard for trade. *Wall Street Journal May, 5*, 1–4.

Greenwood, J., & Jovanovic, B. (1999). The information-technology revolution and the stock market. *American Economic Review, 89*(2), 116–122.

Hagiu, A. (2014). Strategic decisions for multisided platforms. *MIT Sloan Management Review, 55*(2), 71–80.

Hajli, N., & Lin, X. (2016). Exploring the security of information sharing on social networking sites: The role of perceived control of information. *Journal of Business Ethics, 133*(1), 111–123.

Hargittai, E. (2002). Second-level digital divide: Differences in people's online skills. *First Monday, 7*(4), 1–19.

Herhalt, J. (2011). Cyber crime: A growing challenge for governments. *KPMG International: Issues Monitor-Government on Cyber Crime, 8*, 1–24.

Hindman, M. (2018). *The internet trap: How the digital economy builds monopolies and undermines democracy*. Princeton University Press.

Hobijn, B., & Jovanovic, B. (2001). The information-technology revolution and the stock market: Evidence. *American Economic Review, 91*(5), 1203–1220. https://doi.org/10.1257/aer.91.5.1203

Hoofnagle, C. J., van der Sloot, B., & Borgesius, F. Z. (2019). The European Union general data protection regulation: What it is and what it means. *Information & Communications Technology Law, 28*(1), 65–98.

Howard, P. N. (2010). *The digital origins of dictatorship and democracy: Information technology and political Islam*. Oxford University Press.

Hull, C. E. K., Hung, Y. T. C., Hair, N., Perotti, V., & DeMartino, R. (2007). Taking advantage of digital opportunities: A typology of digital entrepreneurship. *International Journal of Networking and Virtual Organisations, 4*(3), 290–303.

Hyrynsalmi, S., Suominen, A., & Mäntymäki, M. (2016). The influence of developer multi-homing on competition between software ecosystems. *Journal of Systems and Software, 111*, 119–127.

Isaak, J., & Hanna, M. J. (2018). User data privacy: Facebook, Cambridge Analytica, and privacy protection. *Computer, 51*(8), 56–59.

Isenberg, D. J. (2010). How to start an entrepreneurial revolution. *Harvard Business Review, 88*(6), 40–50.

Johnson, M. (2016). *Cyber crime, security and digital intelligence*. Routledge.

Jovanovic, B. (1982). Selection and the evolution of industry. *Econometrica, 50*(3), 649–670. https://doi.org/10.2307/1912606

Jovanovic, B. (2001). New technology and the small firm. *Small Business Economics, 16*(1), 53–56. https://doi.org/10.1023/A:1011132809150

Jullien, B. (2012). Two-sided B to B platforms. In M. Peitz & J. Waldfogel (Eds.), *The Oxford handbook of the digital economy* (pp. 61–85). Oxford University Press.

Kane, G. C., Palmer, D., Nguyen-Phillips, A., Kiron, D., & Buckley, N. (2017). Achieving digital maturity. *MIT Sloan Management Review, 59*(1), 1–32.

Kenney, M., & Zysman, J. (2016). The rise of the platform economy. *Issues in Science and Technology, 32*(3), 61.

Kiiski, S., & Pohjola, M. (2002). Cross-country diffusion of the internet. *Information Economics and Policy, 14*(2), 297–310.

Kirzner, I. M. (2015). *Competition and entrepreneurship*. University of Chicago Press.

Klang, M., & Murray, A. (Eds.). (2005). *Human rights in the digital age*. Psychology Press.

Kokolakis, S. (2017). Privacy attitudes and privacy behaviour: A review of current research on the privacy paradox phenomenon. *Computers & Security, 64*, 122–134.

Kummer, M., & Schulte, P. (2019). When private information settles the bill: Money and privacy in Google's market for smartphone applications. *Management Science, 65*(8), 3470–3494.

Kundi, G. M., & Akhtar, R. (2014). Digital revolution, cyber-crimes and cyber legislation: A challenge to governments in developing countries. *Journal of Information Engineering and Applications, 4*(4), 61–71.

Lafuente, E., Acs, Z. J., Sanders, M., & Szerb, L. (2020). The global technology frontier: Productivity growth and the relevance of Kirznerian and Schumpeterian entrepreneurship. *Small Business Economics, 55*, 153–178.

Lampson, B. W. (2004). Computer security in the real world. *Computer, 37*(6), 37–46.

Lee, C. S. (2001). An analytical framework for evaluating e-commerce business models and strategies. *Internet Research, 11*(4), 349–359.

Li, W., Badr, Y., & Biennier, F. (2012). Digital ecosystems: Challenges and prospects. In proceedings of the international conference on management of emergent digital EcoSystems (pp. 117–122). MEDES'12. https://doi.org/10.1145/2457276.2457297.

Lund, J., & Ebbesson, E. (2019). Understanding digital innovation from a layered architectural perspective. *Technology Innovation Management Review, 9*(2), 51–63.

Lyytinen, K., Yoo, Y., & Boland, R. J., Jr. (2016). Digital product innovation within four classes of innovation networks. *Information Systems Journal, 26*(1), 47–75.

Malecki, E. J. (2018). Entrepreneurship and entrepreneurial ecosystems. *Geography Compass, 12*(3), e12359. https://doi.org/10.1111/gec3.12359

McIntyre, D. P., & Srinivasan, A. (2017). Networks, platforms, and strategy: Emerging views and next steps. *Strategic Management Journal, 38*(1), 141–160.

Milner, H. V. (2006). The digital divide: The role of political institutions in technology diffusion. *Comparative Political Studies, 39*(2), 176–199.

Monsellato, A. (2016). Tesla Motors: a business model innovation in the automotive industry http://tesi.luiss.it/16605/1/659181.pdf

Moore, M., & Tambini, D. (Eds.). (2018). *Digital dominance: The power of Google, Amazon, Facebook, and apple*. Oxford University Press.

Morgan, S. (2018). Fake news, disinformation, manipulation and online tactics to undermine democracy. *Journal of Cyber Policy, 3*(1), 39–43.

Murawski, M., & Bick, M. (2017). Digital competences of the workforce: A research topic? *Business Process Management Journal, 23*(3), 721–734.

Nambisan, S. (2017). Digital entrepreneurship: Toward a digital technology perspective of entrepreneurship. *Entrepreneurship Theory and Practice, 41*(6), 1029–1055. https://doi.org/10.1111/etap.12254

Naudé, W. (2016). *Is European entrepreneurship in crisis? IZA working paper, DP 9817*. IZA Institute for Labor Economics.

Njenga, J. K. (2018). Digital literacy: The quest of an inclusive definition. *Reading & Writing, 9*(1), 1–7.

Nuechterlein, J. E., & Weiser, P. J. (2007). *Digital crossroads: American telecommunications policy in the internet age*. MIT Press Books.

Parker, G., & Van Alstyne, M. (2014). Platform strategy. In M. Augier & D. Teece (Eds.), *Palgrave encyclopedia of strategic management*. Palgrave MacMillan.

Pasquier, T., Singh, J., Powles, J., Eyers, D., Seltzer, M., & Bacon, J. (2018). Data provenance to audit compliance with privacy policy in the internet of things. *Personal and Ubiquitous Computing, 22*(2), 333–344.

Peitz, M., & Waldfogel, J. (Eds.). (2012). *The Oxford handbook of the digital economy*. Oxford University Press.

Persily, N. (2017). The 2016 US election: Can democracy survive the internet? *Journal of Democracy, 28*(2), 63–76.

Peters, M. A., & Roberts, P. (2015). *Virtues of openness: Education, science, and scholarship in the digital age*. Routledge.

Poore, M. (2015). *Using social media in the classroom: A best practice guide*. Sage.

Prensky, M. (2009). H. sapiens digital: From digital immigrants and digital natives to digital wisdom. *Innovate: Journal of online. Education, 5*(3), 1–9.

Robinson, L., Cotten, S., Ono, H., Quan-Haase, A., Mesch, G., Chen, W., Schulz, J., Hale, T., & Stern, M. (2015). Digital inequalities and why they matter. *Information, Communication & Society, 18*(5), 569–582. https://doi.org/10.1080/1369118X.2015.1012532

Roca, C. J., García, J., & de la Vega, J. (2009). The importance of perceived trust, security and privacy in online trading systems. *Information Management & Computer Security, 17*(2), 96–113.

Rochet, J. C., & Tirole, J. (2003). Platform competition in two-sided markets. *Journal of the European Economic Association, 1*(4), 990–1029.

Rochet, J.-C., & Tirole, J. (2006). Two-sided markets: A progress report. *The Rand Journal of Economics, 37*(3), 645–667. https://doi.org/10.1111/j.1756-2171.2006.tb00036.x

Root, H. L. (2020). *Network origins of the global economy*. Cambridge University Press.

Rose, J. (2017). Brexit, trump, and post-truth politics. *Public Integrity: American Society for Public Administration, 19*(6), 555–558. https://doi.org/10.1080/10999922.2017.1285540

Rosenzweig, P., Bucci, S. P., & Inserra, D. (2017). Next steps for US cybersecurity in the trump administration: Active cyber defense. *Background, 3188*, 11.

Saadatmand, F., Lindgren, R., & Schultze, U. (2019). Configurations of platform organizations: Implications for complementor engagement. *Research Policy, 48*(8), 103770. https://doi.org/10.1016/j.respol.2019.03.015

Sahut, J.-M., Iandoli, L., & Teulon, F. (2019). The age of digital entrepreneurship. *Small Business Economics., 56*, 1159–1169. https://doi.org/10.1007/s11187-019-00260-8

Scheerder, A., van Deursen, A., & van Dijk, J. (2017). Determinants of internet skills, uses and outcomes: A systematic review of the second- and third-level digital divide. *Telematics and Informatics, 34*(8), 1607–1624.

Schumpeter, J. A. (1934). *The theory of economic development: An inquiry into profits. Capital, credit, interest and the business cycle* (2nd ed.). Harvard University Press.

Shannon, C. (1948). A mathematical theory of communication. *Bell Systems Technical Journal, 27*(3), 379–423.

Shapiro, C., & Varian, H. (1999). *Information rules*. Harvard Business School Press.

Smith, H. J., Dinev, T., & Xu, H. (2011). Information privacy research: An interdisciplinary review. *MIS Quarterly, 35*(4), 989–1016.

Song, A. K. (2019). The digital entrepreneurial ecosystem: A critique and reconfiguration. *Small Business Economics, 53*(3), 569–590. https://doi.org/10.1007/s11187-019-00232-y

Spigel, B. (2017). The relational organization of entrepreneurial ecosystems. *Entrepreneurship Theory and Practice, 41*(1), 49–72.

Stam, E. (2015). Entrepreneurial ecosystems and regional policy: A sympathetic critique. *European Planning Studies, 23*(9), 1759–1769. https://doi.org/10.1080/09654313.2015.1061484

Steininger, D. M. (2019). Linking information systems and entrepreneurship: A review and agenda for IT-associated and digital entrepreneurship research. *Information Systems Journal, 29*(2), 363–407.

Sussan, F., & Acs, Z. J. (2017). The digital entrepreneurial ecosystem. *Small Business Economics, 49*(1), 55–73. https://doi.org/10.1007/s11187-017-9867-5

Szerb, L., Lafuente, E., Horváth, K., & Páger, B. (2019). The relevance of quantity and quality entrepreneurship for regional performance: The moderating role of the entrepreneurial ecosystem. *Regional Studies, 53*(9), 1308–1320.

Tura, N., Kutvonen, A., & Ritala, P. (2018). Platform design framework: Conceptualisation and application. *Technology Analysis & Strategic Management, 30*(8), 881–894.

Van Dijk, J. A. (2017). *Digital divide: Impact of access. The International Encyclopedia of Media Effects* (pp. 1–11). Wiley. https://doi.org/10.1002/9781118783764.wbieme0043

Voogt, J., & Roblin, N. P. (2012). A comparative analysis of international frameworks for 21st century competences: Implications for national curriculum policies. *Journal of Curriculum Studies, 44*(3), 299–321.

Weeks, B. E., & Gil de Zúñiga, H. (2019). What's next? Six observations for the future of political misinformation research. *American Behavioral Scientist, 65*(2), 277–289.

Weidmann, N. B., Benitez-Baleato, S., Hunziker, P., Glatz, E., & Dimitropoulos, X. (2016). Digital discrimination: Political bias in internet service provision across ethnic groups. *Science, 353*(6304), 1151–1155.

Weill, P., & Woerner, S. L. (2015). Thriving in an increasingly digital ecosystem. *MIT Sloan Management Review, 56*(4), 27.

Wentrup, R., & Ström, P. (2017). Online service providers: A new and unique species of the firm? In M. Taddeo & L. Floridi (Eds.), *The responsibilities of online service providers* (pp. 157–177). Springer.

West, D. M. (2015). *Digital divide: Improving internet access in the developing world through affordable services and diverse content*. Brookings Institution.

Weyl, E. G. (2010). A price theory of multi-sided platforms. *American Economic Review, 100*(4), 1642–1672.

Whitman, M., & Mattord, H. (2012). *Principles of information security*. Cengage Learning.

Williams, J. (2003). *The skills for life survey: A national needs and impact survey of literacy, numeracy and ICT skills* (No. 490). The Stationery Office.

The manufacturer's authorised representative in the EU is Springer Nature Customer Service Centre GmbH, Europaplatz 3, 69115 Heidelberg, Germany. If you have any concerns regarding our products, please contact ProductSafety@springernature.com

Printed and bound by CPI Group (UK) Ltd, Croydon, CR0 4YY
30/09/2026
02225606-0006